BORODIN AND LISZT

AMS PRESS
NEW YORK

A. de Borodine
St. Pétersbourg

Frontispiece.

BORODIN AND LISZT

I.

Life and Works of a Russian Composer

II.

Liszt, as Sketched in the Letters of Borodin

BY

ALFRED HABETS

Translated with a Preface by

ROSA NEWMARCH

With Portraits and Fac-similes

LONDON

DIGBY, LONG & CO., PUBLISHERS

18 BOUVERIE STREET, FLEET STREET, E.C.

Library of Congress Cataloging in Publication Data

Habets, Alfred, 1839-1908.
    Borodin and Liszt.

    Translation of Alexandre Borodine, d'après la
biographie et la correspondence publiées par Wladimir
Stassoff.
    Reprint of the 1895 ed. published by Digby, Long,
London.
    CONTENTS: Life and works of a Russian composer—
Liszt, as sketched in the letters of Borodin.
    1. Borodin, Aleksandr Porfir'evich, 1834-1887.
2. Composers—Russia—Biography. 3. Liszt, Franz,
1811-1886.
ML410.B73H13   1977   780'.92'4 [B]   74-24093
ISBN 0-404-12938-2

From the edition of 1895, London
First AMS edition published in 1977
Manufactured in the United States of America

AMS PRESS INC.
NEW YORK, N.Y.

CONTENTS

————o————

		PAGE
Translator's Preface,	.	ix
Preface,	.	xlix
I. A Double Vocation,	.	1
II. The Scientist,	.	13
III. The Artist. His First Compositions,	.	20
IV. Balakireff and his School,	.	26
V. Dramatic Works—Prince Igor—Mlada, .	.	34
VI. The Libretto of Prince Igor, .	.	39
VII. The Score of Prince Igor. Second Symphony,	.	46
VIII. Visits to Belgium. Success Abroad,	.	66
IX. Death of Borodin. Posthumous Works,	.	88
X. The Man,	.	93

Preface to Second Part,		.	103
I. Letter to Madame Borodin, Jena, July 3d, 1877, .			107
II. Do.,	Do.,	Jena, July 12th, 1877, .	130
III. Do.,	Do.,	Jena, July 18th, 1877, .	142
IV. Do.,	Do.,	Marburg, July 22d, 1877,	153
V. Fragment of a Letter to César Cui, Magdeburg, June 12th, 1881, .			160
VI. Letter to Madame Borodin, Weimar, June 19th, 1881,			185

TRANSLATOR'S PREFACE

—o—

In little more than a year, death has removed the two most prominent figures in the musical world of Russia. In October 1893, Tschaïkowsky conducted the first performance in St Petersburg of his symphony in B minor, op. 74, to which he gave the predictive title of "Symphonie Pathétique." When three weeks later the work was repeated by the Imperial Musical Society, the occasion was an "In Memoriam" concert, given in honour of the composer himself; in the short interval, Tschaïkowsky had fallen a victim to the cholera. On November 20th, 1894, his more

renowned fellow-countryman, Anton Rubinstein, passed suddenly from among us.   These
two musicians, the former for many years
director of the Conservatoire at Moscow, the
latter, the founder and head of the sister
institution in St Petersburg, had exercised
for a considerable period an almost auto-
cratic influence over the musical life of
Russia.

In an article in the *Revue de Belgique* in
1885, entitled " Souvenirs d'un Voyage en
Russie : Impressions Musicales," Monsieur A.
Habets relates with considerable humour the
results of a pilgrimage to Russia, undertaken
with the hope of hearing Russian music.   Nothing, apparently, could have been more fruit-
less than his quest for the genuine article.   He
found that the Russian music he had heard
applauded at the Trocadéro during the Paris
Exhibition of 1878, awakened only a half-
hearted enthusiasm at home.   Had he visited
St Petersburg some eighteen years earlier, he
would have witnessed the triumphant reception
accorded to Berlioz, whose music found scant
favour in his native capital.   Such are the re-

venges of time. In the Isaac Cathedral Monsieur Habets was profoundly impressed with the touching and characteristic music of the Greek ritual, and with the *à capella* singing of the famous choir. He also made acquaintance with some of the popular songs of southern Russia, and these experiences strengthened his conviction that a people possessed of a church music so emotional, and a folk-music so captivating, so picturesque and racy of the soil, must have produced composers capable of moulding its wealth of national melody into some permanent and beautiful art forms. Such a school of musicians did indeed exist; he heard them referred to occasionally, though often in terms of depreciation or total misconception. During his visit to St Petersburg he was introduced into a Russian family, for the purpose of discussing the musical question with a man of taste. His informant turned out to be a young and fashionable *dilettante*. One cannot help speculating as to what would be the impression of English music which a total stranger might gather from a similar interview in a

London drawing-room.   Would he be told
that we had no serious and representative
composers worth discussion ?   Or learn that
English music found its only true expression
in the comic operas of Sir Arthur Sullivan ?
Would he be taken to the Symphony Concerts
or to the Music Halls ?   In short, would it
be to Dr Hubert Parry, or to Mr Albert
Chevalier, that he would be bidden to pay
homage as the immediate representative of
musical modernity in England ?   We can but
conjecture and pity the confusion of mind
which would be almost certain to result from
this method of picking up information on the
spot.   The summing up of the Russian amateur was succinct, if one-sided :—" Orchestral
works by composers of the New School are
occasionally given, but meet with poor success.
Tschaïkowsky is our most truly national glory.
He and Rubinstein alone represent modern
music in Russia."   This being a sample of
public opinion in St Petersburg itself, it is
scarcely surprising if foreigners believe that
with the quenching of these two lights music
in Russia has suffered a total eclipse.   Yet

this is far from being the case. There exist
in Russia other musical forces, hardly reckoned
with at home, and very imperfectly gauged by
the outer world. It would be idle to deny
the worth and importance of Tschaïkowsky
and Rubinstein, but it would be equally unjust
to accept them as the sole representatives of
Russian music. What they have actually
represented in Russia has been classical tradition and German tendencies, and their influence, on the whole, has been inimical to
that independent circle whose chief aim has
been to embody in musical form all that is
most worthy in the national temperament.
These men, with their frankly progressive
and nationalist programme, whose works, in
the words of Liszt, " are well worth the serious
attention of musical Europe," form the New
School of Russian music, of which Borodin was
a leading spirit. His biography, which now
appears in English dress, throws many interesting side lights upon the evolution of this
school ; but its origin is so interesting, its
work—during a comparatively short existence
of some five-and-thirty years—so remarkable,

both in quantity and quality, that we may be pardoned for dwelling on the circumstances which led to its foundation. To rightly estimate its importance as a national movement, it is essential to give some account of musical progess in Russia.

It was late before the creative inspiration visited Russia. If we turn to the close of the last century, we shall find that her music, like her literature and general culture, was a purely foreign importation. Of course, we are now speaking of music as a fine art, for the folk-music of Russia, with its reflection of Oriental modes and capricious freedom of rhythm — characteristics which lend themselves to great diversity of emotional expression—is almost unequalled in wealth and variety. It was not until 1735 that, at the desire of the Empress Anne, an Italian opera company first visited St Petersburg, under the management of Francesco Araya, a composer of some reputation in his day. During the reign of Elisabeth an important step was taken towards the institution of a national opera—namely, the formation of a company of

Russian singers who sang in their native tongue. The Empress Catherine II. carried still further the work which had been started by her predecessors, and under her government several operas by native composers were put on the stage. The best known of these musicians were Volkoff, Alabieff, Verstowski — the composer of a popular opera, "The Tomb of Askold"—and Cavos, a Russian by adoption only. But though in the works of the two last there seems to have been some faint reflection of national colour, in all the rest the text only was Russian, the music retaining its purely Italian character.

A native composer of genius, destined to carry out a great work, did appear, however, during this reign. The Imperial Cathedral Choir, afterwards to become celebrated throughout Europe, consisted of about 100 singers, trained to perform the unaccompanied music of the Greek ritual. The soprano and alto parts were taken by boys who were often brought from Southern Russia, where the milder climate is more favourable to the

development of the voice. These boys remained in the choir until their voices broke,
when they were drafted into the employment
of the government, or, if their vocal powers
returned, permitted to re-enter the Cathedral
service. In the time of Catherine II. one of
these choristers attracted the attention of the
authorities by his remarkable gift for composition. This boy, a native of Ukraine,
where he was born in 1751, was Dimitri
Bortniansky. By the generosity of his
Imperial Mistress, Bortniansky was sent to
complete his musical education in Italy under
the celebrated composer Galuppi. On his
return to St Petersburg, being appointed
director of the Imperial Choir, he resolved to
achieve a complete reformation in the music
of the Greek Church. Bortniansky enriched
the Cathedral ritual by settings of no fewer
than fifty psalms, for four and eight voices, a
mass for three voices and several versions of
the Te Deum. For his services rendered to
the music of the Eastern Church he has been
called "the Russian Palestrina." He died in
1825.

Bortniansky was the first Russian musician of considerable genius, but he left no immediate successors. The time had not yet come for the foundation of a school. He was succeeded as director of the Imperial Choir by Theodore von Lvoff, a talented and enthusiastic musician, well fitted to maintain the standard of excellence attained by his predecessor. His most useful work was the publication of the many MSS. which Bortniansky had bequeathed to the Choir. So far, these compositions had been unknown outside St Petersburg, but they were now placed within reach of the whole Greek Church and became an accepted portion of its ritual. In 1836, Theodore von Lvoff was followed by his more celebrated brother, Alexis. Alexis von Lvoff, besides being director of the Imperial Choir, was a distinguished officer of engineers, held the rank of general, and was personal aide-de-camp to the Emperor Nicholas. He was the son of a wealthy landed proprietor, and was born at Reval in 1799. His love of music showed itself at an early age. At seven he began to learn the violin, and made such rapid progress that at the end of a year he could take part in a quartet and play some of the easier concertos very creditably.   In spite of the interruptions caused by his military career, he managed to keep up his favourite pursuit and to become an efficient performer. He cultivated chamber-music most assiduously, and won the reputation of being a first-rate leader of quartets.   Lvoff composed several fantasias for violin and orchestra, besides motets and military marches.   His most important works were an opera " Ondine " and a "Stabat Mater," both of considerable merit. He is best known, however, as the composer of the Russian National Hymn.   Under his management the Imperial Chapel of Court Singers attained to a very high degree of discipline and cultivation.   They were second only to the celebrated Sistine Choir.   Berlioz, in his letters to von Lvoff, pays more than one tribute to their artistic excellence.   Writing from London in January 1848,* after making some disparaging remarks upon musical taste in England, and complaining of the

* *Life and Letters of Berlioz.*   Letter xxxix. Vol. I. p. 180.

want of discipline in Jullien's band, which
he was then conducting at Drury Lane, he
says :—

"Oh, Russia! with its cordial hospitality,
its literary and artistic manners, the organisation of its theatres and its chapel, that precise,
clearly-defined, inflexible organisation without
which, in music as in many other things,
nothing good and nothing beautiful can be
done—who will give me back all this? Why
are you so far away?"

Again, in a letter dated two years later, he
refers to the profound impression left in his
mind by the performances of the Russian
musicians :—"It will always be a pleasure to
me to keep the few sober readers we have in
Paris informed of the great and serious things
that are being done in Russia. . . . Remember me to your wonderful Chapel, and
tell the artists belonging to it that I would
fain listen to them, if only to draw forth the
tears I feel scalding within me and falling on
my heart."

Up to this time the musical life of St
Petersburg had been full of activity, but the

impulse tended more to performance and appreciation than to actual creation. Among foreign musicians then resident in the Russian capital were Wilhelm Lenz, the biographer of Beethoven, the English pianist and composer, John Field, Henri Romberg, Tajan-Rogé and Guillon. Among a host of distinguished visitors were Liszt and Berlioz. Thus it will be seen that all that munificent patronage, enthusiastic cultivation, fostering care and the possession of a fine executive body could do to further the progress of music in Russia had been accomplished; and now the one thing lacking—a native leader—was to appear upon the scene. Michael Ivanovitch Glinka, the founder of the modern national school, the "Patriarch-Prophet of music in Russia," was born in 1804, in the government of Smolensk. As a child he showed a precocious talent for music, and the circumstances of his early life were favourable to its development. His uncle, a wealthy landowner, kept a private band, after the fashion of the day, and little Michael, when visiting his relative, found his greatest pleasure in listening to these musicians. Thus his enthusiasm for music, and especially for the highly-coloured stimulating music of his own country, was first awakened. Soon he took part in their performances, and even attempted to compose something for them. At thirteen Glinka began his education in St Petersburg. He possessed the versatile intellect, so interesting a characteristic of the Slavic race, which is so often fatal to supreme excellence in any one direction. Glinka's college career was brilliant. He became a first-rate linguist, and added a special knowledge of geography and zoology to his many accomplishments. Neither was his musical education neglected; he took piano lessons from Field, and studied theory with Dehn. Before he was twenty-five he published some variations for harp and piano, a string quartet and a few songs. About this time he went to Italy and remained there for four years; but this sojourn, though undertaken at an impressionable period of his life, does not seem to have left many traces on his subsequent work. Probably he was already too deeply

imbued with the characteristic folk-music of
his own country to be in danger of losing
his individuality in the colourless musical
atmosphere of Italy where, at the period of
his visit, the stereotyped and the inane held
undisputed dominion.   Glinka was destined
for a national poet, and, as in the case of
Chopin, exile rather deepened than obliterated
the early impressions of his native music.   On
his return to Russia he began to compose the
national opera which was to make so direct an
appeal to the hearts of his countrymen.
"Life for the Czar" was performed in St
Petersburg for the first time on October 9th,
1836.   Glinka had not miscalculated his
power to awaken patriotic enthusiasm by
means of a genuine Russian opera.   Its
success was immediate and unprecedented ;
Glinka passed into fame and popularity and
became the hero of the hour.   A literary and
artistic *coterie* rallied round him, and his
influence seemed to give a new life to Russian
culture.   He was appointed director of the
Imperial Chapel, but did not continue long in
office.   His health was always delicate, and

he was disposed to be hypochondriacal, which made all routine work particularly distasteful to him.

In spite of certain obvious defects, the vivacity, melodic charm and local colour so happily introduced in the music of "Life for the Czar," had carried all before it; but Glinka had yet to experience the capricious nature of the popular taste. In 1842 he completed his second opera, "Russian and Ludmilla," the subject of which is adapted from a poem by Pushkin. The libretto of "Russlan and Ludmilla" must have been a curious example of literary patchwork, for Cui says that Glinka employed no less than five authors, who worked independently and without definite plan. But whatever may have been the demerits of the text, the music of this opera has been pronounced by Liszt and Berlioz as far in advance of that of "Life for the Czar." Yet the audience, who had received his early work with unbounded approbation, accorded only a chilly welcome to the fruit of his matured genius. "Russlan," neglected by the public, and reproached by the critics, was not heard

again until fifteen years after its first production. The effect of this sudden change
in the popular temper could not but be galling
to a nature of such extreme sensibility as
Glinka's. For a time it seemed as though the
springs of his inspiration were frozen. He
left St Petersburg and betook himself to Paris
in 1844. Later on he visited Spain; there,
under the influence of southern skies, his
creative impulse was stirred anew and he
composed his "Jota Aragonesa," a work in
which Liszt delighted, and which displays to
the full his piquant originality and elegant
workmanship. On his return to Russia he
wrote a symphonic poem, "Une Nuit à Madrid."
A symphonic piece, based upon national airs,
inspired by Gogol's celebrated novel, *Tarass
Boulba*, and a third opera, "Le Bigame,"
were left uncompleted at the time of his
death, which occurred at Berlin, February 2d,
1827.

Widely different, in character and inspiration, from the works just mentioned are those
of Dargomijsky, for whom, however, many of
his compatriots claim equal honours with

Glinka. Dargomijsky's parentage, and the
circumstances of his childhood, were much the
same as those of Glinka, and in his case, too,
comparative affluence enabled him to devote
himself freely to the cultivation of music.
But there all analogy ceases. Glinka travelled much, became acquainted with the great
musical lights of his day, and won for his
compositions a certain measure of appreciation outside his own country. Dargomijsky,
on the contrary, spent his whole life in St
Petersburg, and deep as are the traces of his
influence upon the music of his compatriots,
his name is almost unknown in Western
Europe. Yet, in spite of his isolation and
home life, the national element seems never
to have had the same powerful attraction for
Dargomijsky that it had for Glinka. His
earliest essays in composition, like those of
so many of the Russian composers, seem to
have been somewhat amateurish. It was not
until he came in contact with Glinka that
his enthusiasm for dramatic music was
awakened and he began to work in earnest.
His first choice of a subject fell upon Victor

Hugo's poem "Esmeralda." This work he submitted to the directors of the Imperial theatres in 1839. After waiting eight years for a definite answer, Dargomijsky at last had the satisfaction of seeing "Esmeralda" performed at Moscow. His opera, "The Roussalka" ("The River Nymph"), taken from Pushkin's celebrated poem, was accepted by the Imperial directors in 1856. At first it met with poor success, but in later years it came to be better appreciated, and is now an established favourite with the public. The subject of "The Roussalka," which is weird and highly romantic, seems better suited to the genius of a Weber than to the realistic temperament of Dargomijsky. In imaginative qualities he is somewhat lacking, though endowed with great dramatic power and a command of grotesque humour. Dargomijsky is essentially a master of declamation; a rhetorical rather than a musical genius, to whom a just dramatic expression is the first consideration. He has not the personal inspiration, the wealth of graceful and spontaneous melody, the command of musical

science which were Glinka's special gifts. It
seems probable that he will be remembered
more for what he had the courage to undo
than for what he actually created. His
predilection for melodic recitative and the
various innovating tendencies characteristic
of his style are already apparent in "The
Roussalka"; but it is only in his third and
last opera, "The Stone Guest," that his
progressive principles appear in full maturity.
This music-drama, which is considered by Cui
to be the most advanced and remarkable
work of the new Russian School, is based on
the same subject as Mozart's masterpiece.
This seems in itself a challenge of all tradition, and savours of revolutionary audacity.
But we must bear in mind that Dargomijsky
found his subject ready to hand in the well-
known poem by Pushkin. In many respects
the Russian version differs essentially from
Da Ponte's libretto of "Don Juan." The
poem, notwithstanding its literary merits,
offers extreme difficulties to a musical
setting. For instance, throughout the whole
work there is no logical opportunity for the

introduction of a chorus. Lenz describes this opera as a "recitative in three acts," broken only by a charming song for Laura (a character who does not appear in Mozart's "Don Juan"), which is Spanish in colouring and has the rhythm of a cachuca. At Dargomijsky's death this work, though completely sketched out, was unfinished as regards instrumentation. Its completion was undertaken by Rimsky-Korsakoff* and Cui, to whose devoted efforts is mainly due the representation of the work after the composer s death.

We have given some account of the two composers who may be regarded as the creators of modern music in Russia, but any review of the subject would be incomplete without a brief reference to another musician who, though of Russian origin, owes his inspiration more directly to Wagner than to Glinka or Dargomijsky. Alexander Séroff was born at St Petersburg in 1820. His

---

* In writing the names of Korsakoff, Balakireff and Glazounoff, the Translator has adopted the termination most familiar to English readers ; but on the authority of Monsieur Habets, Korsakow, Balakirew, etc., would be the correct orthography.

musical abilities developed somewhat late in life, and seemed to be rather of the critical than of the constructive order. He made some reputation as a writer on musical subjects before he ventured into the sphere of dramatic composition. In 1860, after seeing Ristori in a performance of "Judith," he conceived the idea of composing an opera on the same subject. Séroff was undoubtedly master of all the technicalities of his art, but no ingenuity could atone for his lack of real inspiration. "Judith" was followed by a second work, "The Evil Power" ("La Force Maligne"). Both operas display some vigour of conception and a certain showy musical eloquence, but are marred by a coarse realism and want of sensibility. Cui says that in "Judith" he has given us "a companion-picture to 'l'Assommoir,' fifteen years before the advent of naturalistic literature." In his lack of refinement and disregard of poetic charm, Séroff was the antithesis of Glinka who, like Chopin, was one of the patricians of music.

We have now come to the foundation of the contemporary school itself. In 1856 two

young men, Balakireff and Cæsar Cui, met
in St Petersburg and were drawn together
by the love of music which they had in
common. Round these two enthusiastic spirits
flocked a little band of fellow-workers —
Rimsky - Korsakoff, Moussorgsky, and later
on, Borodin. The dream of this friendly
league was the emancipation of their art
from subserviency to foreign interests and
the institution of a national school of
music. There is a considerable similarity
in aim and origin between this association
and our own pre-Raphaelite brotherhood.
For peace and good-fellowship, we do not
think it has any parallel in musical history.
Often we must admire the devotion with
which its members worked for one another,
as, for instance, after the death of Dargomijsky, Moussorgsky and Borodin. Admirable,
too, is the spirit in which criticism, often of
a very unsparing character, seems to have
been given and taken among the brethren.
In this little circle the musical questions of
the day were discussed, plans formed, the
artistic impulse awakened and kept at

tension. But something more than stimulating intercourse and æsthetic talk was
aimed at. By degrees definite principles
were formulated and communicated to others,
so justifying the claims of the association
to be called a " School " in the true sense of
the word. This high level has been main-
tained, for even after the first heat of enthusiasm had partially cooled, the organisation
never degenerated into a clique for the advance-
ment of private interests and the offering of
incense at particular shrines. We will give
in condensed form the principles of art as set
forth by the Russian School, keeping as nearly
as possible to the words of Cui himself :—

(1) *Dramatic music must always possess
an intrinsic value as absolute music, even when
taken apart from the text.* (2) *The vocal music
should be in perfect accordance with the mean-
ing of the text.* (3) *The scenes of which an
opera is composed must be entirely dependent
upon the relations between the characters, as
well as upon the general action of the piece.*

Besides these chief tenets of their musical
creed, the Russian school lays great stress

upon the literary worth of the libretto, the musical portrayal of character, a due regard for the historical period of a drama, and a judicious employment of local colour.

These principles, according to Cui, are closely allied to those of Wagner; but the methods of attaining the same ends differ essentially in the two schools. While Wagner concentrates the whole musical interest in the orchestra, entrusting to it the representative themes of certain characters, the Russians reserve the most important musical phrases for the singers, whom they make the real interpreters of the composer's intention. That is to say, if we may borrow the words of Grétry to Napoleon, they put the statue upon the stage and the pedestal in the orchestra. Thus it will be seen that the Russian school claims its descent from Glinka and Dargomijsky rather than from Wagner.

It will be obvious, however, to every unprejudiced mind that neither Glinka nor Dargomijsky can claim to have invented these theories which were first exemplified in the masterpieces of Gluck.

A continuous unanimity of opinion and purpose could not be expected from any human organisation. Gradually the law of differentiation asserted itself, and the New School put forth a series of works which varied with the individual tendencies of the composer.

We should like at some future time to put before English readers some longer and more detailed account of the members of this interesting *coterie.* For the present we must limit ourselves to a few words about its chief representatives. Of Balakireff, of whose fascinating personality we get a tantalising glimpse in the letters of Borodin, we regret to have so few details to relate. What we gather concerning him seems significant. The founder and practical teacher of the New School, whose disciples were afterwards to be dubbed musical revolutionaries, realists and even nihilists,* does not appear himself as the upholder of ultra radical principles, but as a thoroughly efficient and erudite musician, well-

---

* "Borodin's music might fairly be termed Nihilistic." Naumann's *History of Music*, p. 1260.

versed in traditional forms, an admirer of the great masters, an "ardent defender of sharps and flats," and interested in all questions of musical science. His instrumentation is, we are told, "of classical correctness." He has composed three overtures on national themes ; a symphonic poem, "Thamar," and a symphonic score to "King Lear," which is considered his masterpiece. His Oriental fantasia for pianoforte, "Islamey," is a work of remarkable interest which demands for its performance an exceptional virtuosity. It was a favourite piece of Liszt's, who often referred to it as Balakireff's charming Oriental rattle.

Cui, who has risen to the rank of General, and is Professor of Fortification at the School of Military Engineering in St Petersburg, adds to his talents as a composer considerable gifts as a writer and critic. In his interesting work, "La Musique en Russie," now, unfortunately, out of print, he appears as the spokesman of the New School. His style is clear and trenchant, his criticism exceedingly outspoken, and his sarcasm has a very keen edge. We take this opportunity of acknowledging that we are largely indebted to his book for much of the information on which this Introduction is based. From the first, Cui was more attracted to dramatic than to symphonic music. He has composed in two distinct styles. His operas, "The Prisoner of the Caucasus" and "The Mandarin's Son," belong to his early period. Afterwards his views of art underwent a radical change, and these works are separated from his later efforts—"William Ratcliffe" (1869) and "Angelo" (1876)—by as wide a gulf as that which divides "Il Trovatore" from "Falstaff." Cui's latest opera, "Le Flibustier," recently performed in Paris, was by no means a success. The work is well constructed, but lacks warmth and vitality.

Rimsky-Korsakoff, who began life as a naval officer, was born in 1844. We are reminded of Pierre Loti, the sailor-author of "Pêcheur d'Islande," when we picture to ourselves this enthusiastic votary of music, who found time on his voyages round the

world to combine composition and a severe
course of theoretical studies with his duties
at the guns or on the quarter-deck. Of all
his musical colleagues, Rimsky-Korsakoff is
the one who has best assimilated the spirit
of his native music. After imbibing the
radical principles of the advanced school, he
underwent a complete reaction and, like
the poet Carducci, plunged into " a cold
bath of erudition." For a time he devoted
himself to the study of the severest forms
of polyphonic art. Rimsky-Korsakoff is the
composer of several operas—" The Snow-
Maiden," " A Night in May," " Mlada,"
etc. But his genius finds its truest expression in his purely instrumental music. His
symphonic sketches, " Sadko " and " Antar,"
musical illustrations of popular legends, are
full of suggestive poetical charm tinged
with Oriental colour ; original alike in conception and orchestral treatment, they are
remarkable specimens of programme music.
Cui, while doing justice to his many qualities,
finds fault with Rimsky-Korsakoff for a
certain lack of " nerve," of " passionate im-

pulse." Perhaps, in truth, he may have moods of languor and passiveness alternating with others of sudden expansion, both equally characteristic of the Slavonic race. Perhaps, too, he may have carried away from his studies in an austere classical atmosphere some imperfectly realised ideal of expression which gives to his style an occasional sense of strain and labour. But whatever may be his weaknesses, we must confess that this composer, who has braced himself with the study of Bach and Beethoven without losing anything of the peculiar and subtle essence of his native music, appeals to us personally as the most attractive individuality in an exceptionally interesting group. Besides the works enumerated, Rimsky - Korsakoff has published by far the best collection of Russian popular songs.

Moussorgsky is the ultra realist of Russian music. His compositions, which are sometimes repellent, but always full of his dominating personality, are of all the works of this school the most antipathetic to

Western taste. His greatest work, the opera
"Boris Godounoff," exemplifies at once his
merits and defects ; a vigorous declamatory
style, great descriptive powers, a lack of
poetry and lyrical charm. There is no
overture or instrumental introduction of any
kind to "Boris Godounoff," and a large
portion of the text of this singular work is
written in prose. Cui describes it as being
neither opera nor music drama, but an
historical chronicle set to music. Through
all his works runs the same vein of sombre
realism. But his realistic atmosphere, though
oppressive, is never sordid. "He has grasped
the passions as well as the humour of the
Russian people, and depicts them with an
art and truth of expression that cannot be
too highly praised." Moussorgsky strikes
the same chord in music as Tourgenieff in
fiction.

In instrumental music Glazounoff continues
to sustain the reputation which he won by
his first quartet, which appeared in his
seventeenth year. It has been followed at
intervals by his overtures on Greek themes,

his symphonic poem "Stenka Razine," an elegy and other minor compositions. Space forbids us to linger over the graceful elegiac works of Davidoff, the chamber-music of the Czech composer Naprawnik, the refined pianoforte pieces of Liadoff and many other lesser products of Russian genius. We must mention the one great practical outcome of the movement which we have described —the establishment of the Free School of Music in St Petersburg. This institution owes its origin mainly to the efforts of Balakireff and his colleague Lomakin. The Free School possesses an excellent orchestra and the finest choral body—outside the churches—in all Russia. Its present head and conductor is Rimsky-Korsakoff. Less fashionable than those of the Imperial Musical Society, the concerts of the Free School do good work in affording an opening for the creations of native composers, which would never be brought to light by the older and more conservative institution.

We have attempted to give in brief outline the history of music in Russia. So far,

little has been written on the subject, and
our too-scanty information has been gleaned
from articles in English and foreign periodicals,
and other works not always accessible to the
general reader.   No detailed criticism has
been aimed at, for the reason that a large
proportion of the works mentioned are only
known to the writer through the medium
of pianoforte scores and arrangements for
two or four hands.   For the benefit of such
of our readers as desire a more intimate
acquaintance with the Russian school, we
may remark that such arrangements are
very numerous and generally in good taste.
A few have been undertaken by Liszt ; others,
as in the case of Borodin's symphonies, have
been the work of the composer himself.   In
view of this obvious drawback to a complete
knowledge of these works, we can only
venture upon a general appreciation of their
scope and tendencies.

   It has been frequently shown that even
among the most notable of Russian composers
scarcely one has been able to maintain himself
by the exclusive exercise of his art.   Only

those lucky enough to possess private means have been able to devote themselves entirely to music. Others, less fortunate, have been obliged to adopt a second profession, or share the fate of the unfortunate composer Dutch, who, after undergoing privations which shortened his life, found himself reduced to conducting the orchestra of a public garden for a bare livelihood. There is only a small market for musical productions in Russia. Throughout that vast empire, so Cui informs us in the book we have quoted so frequently, there exist but six theatres in which a composer might hope to see the production of a new work. These state-directed theatres were for years more favourable to Italian than to Russian music. Indeed, the patronage of foreign art at the expense of native talent was carried to such lengths that, until recent years, a law existed making it illegal for a Russian musician to receive more than £160 for an opera ; though no such restriction was enforced as regards alien composers. These conditions have had a twofold influence upon Russian art. A stigma of *dilettantism* has

attached itself to some Russian composers
which, when we consider their immature and
tentative efforts at composition, is not perhaps
entirely without justification. But considerable allowance must be made for the fact that
many of them started as amateurs, and at
the outset of life were unable to give more
than a half-hearted attention to an art that
makes the most jealous and insatiable demands
upon its devotees. We cannot gather grapes of
thorns, nor figs of thistles; nor do we expect
from our budding doctors and guardsmen
musical works of serious import, such as some
of the early works of Borodin and Moussorgsky
may fairly claim to be.   In other respects, this
enforcement of a dual career is wholly advantageous to the cause of art. It is a common
idea that genius, before it can give forth its
purest gold, must pass through the fiery trials
of distress and disappointment; and to illus-
trate the assumption that easy circumstances
lead to shallowness of sentiment, people are
fond of pointing to the works of Mendelssohn.
Yet, on the other hand, " slow rises worth by
poverty depressed," and it would be just as

easy to multiply instances where genius combined with worldly independence has produced the finest work in art and literature. One case occurs to us at the moment—Velasquez, the undisputed master of his craft, the most "professional" of painters, enjoyed not only immunity from privation, but a post of dignity and emolument in a king's palace, and rarely, if ever, painted for money. The composer who draws his income from some other source than music, has at least the advantage of a free hand in creation. Where there are no concert-agents to defer to, no musical monopolists to make or mar the ambitious composer, no great half-educated public to cater for, and few posts open to competition, the temptation to write for anything but art's sake is practically *nil*. There is no need for the musician to adapt to the circumstances of his own case Pope's mocking advice to the poet, and " for melodies advise with his log roller." Consequently, in Russia the pot-boiler, the *pièce d'occasion*, the academical nullity, the royalty ballad have no existence, or are, at least, imported evils. Russian music is strenuous; it aims high, and, on the whole, maintains its ideal.

Those who look upon the Russians as mere apprentices in art are disposed to deny them, as yet, the mastery of their craft. This is only partially true. Nearly all their best composers display an ample command of the resources of harmony and counterpoint; but often, like children with a new and complicated mechanical toy, they seem at a loss to make the best use of it. Take, for instance, the "Paraphrases" so often mentioned by Borodin. These clever little pieces are, as Liszt has said, a compendium of musical science in the form of a jest. This kind of elaborate trifling seems to possess a special attraction for the musicians of to-day, yet we can no more imagine such humorists as Beethoven and Mozart taking much delight in it, than we can picture the creator of Falstaff penning the post-prandial philosophisings of Mr Grant Allen. We feel, in listening to the "Paraphrases" and all kindred works, that in whatever school the Russians

have acquired their musical science, it is
from the composer of the " Carnival " and
" Papillons " that they have caught the trick
of this somewhat desultory employment of
their powers.   During its short life the Russian school has accomplished much ; it will
achieve still greater things if its disciples
remain true to their original aims.   They
have nothing to learn from the decadent
romanticism of Germany, and everything
to fear from the contamination of their
pure sources of inspiration by the influx
of a diluted foreign element.   The safe-
guard of their originality will be a vigorous
and healthy patriotism, such as produced
a Burns or a Tennyson in literature, and
a Sebastian Bach in music.   Their development, if it is to lead to higher things, must
come from within, for true musical inspiration is innate, and cannot, as people seem
to think, be caught and propagated at certain centres and in certain " methods," like
an endemic disease.   In a word, Russian
music is at its best when it is most itself,
when it retains most of the savour and colour

native to its growth. It has its special weaknesses; formal excellence, precision of thought, a clearly-defined contour, are not the qualities we must expect at present from the music of a race whose home is in that vast region of limitless horizons "where men and ideas are alike nomadic." It has also its compensating charms, if we accept it as an exotic growth of rare interest and beauty exhaling an unaccustomed perfume; expanding, as yet perhaps, from no great depth of root, but superior in vitality to the etiolated flowers of art which are now appearing in countries overshadowed by a great tradition. We should like the music of Russia to be more often heard and more fully appreciated in England. And since we have accepted the music of Dvoràk and Smetana we cannot plead the excuse of its exotic character. It will be many years before Russian opera can bear transplantation, but with the symphonic works of Balakireff, Glazounoff, Rimsky-Korsakoff and Borodin there are no difficulties in the way. Is it too much to hope that time will make us as familiar with the works of these musicians as we are with those of their literary brethren — Tolstoi, Tourgenieff and Dostoievsky ?

PREFACE.

—— *o* ——

A FEW years ago the composers of the New Russian School were hardly known in Russia. What wonder then that they were ignored abroad.

One illustrious Master, however, gave them the appreciation they deserved. Franz Liszt said that "their compositions made amends for the boredom which other works, better known and more highly praised, inflicted on him," and practising what he preached, he annually made room for the Russian School in the programmes of the Allgemeiner Deutscher Musikverein.*

* See our article, " Souvenirs d'un Voyage en Russie : Impressions Musicales," *Revue de Belgique*, 1885.

Outside Germany the propaganda was carried on by a woman to whom the Russian School owes it greatest successes; the Countess Mercy-Argenteau, as we have said, did for modern Russian music what the Marquis de Voguë has done for its contemporary literature. With indefatigable perseverance she strove to popularise such Russian compositions as found place in our symphony concerts; thanks also to her, a great number of vocal compositions have been translated, and finally Russian composers were induced to visit France and Belgium.

In 1885 Borodin took part in the concerts of the Antwerp Exhibition. The following year he returned to Belgium in company with César Cui, to preside at a Russian concert organised by the *Société d'Emulation* of Liége; at the representations of "The Prisoner of the Caucasus" at the Théâtre Royal of Liége; and at the performances of his symphonies at the Popular Concerts in Brussels, and at the Conservatoire at Liége. In 1889 came the turn of Rimsky-Korsakoff and Glazounoff, whose works were applauded at the Trocadéro. Finally, in 1890, Rimsky-Korsakoff visited Brussels once more to conduct a Popular Concert.

The works and the personality of Borodin attracted immediate attention, and to-day there is not a musician who does not consider him unquestionably the head of the New Russian School.

As president of the musical committee of the *Société d'Emulation*, during his visit to Liége, I was brought into daily contact with Borodin, which speedily awoke a sympathy for the man as great as was my admiration for his works.

The general consternation with which the news of the premature death of this great composer was received in St Petersburg, was shared in Belgium by the numerous friends Borodin had left there. The Countess Mercy-Argenteau having called my attention to the biographical notice which Monsieur W. Stassoff, director of Fine Arts at the Imperial Library of St Petersburg, had dedicated to the memory of this great musician, while at the same time he published a portion of his correspondence,[*] we hastened, with the aid of several Russian students at Liége, to make ourselves acquainted with the work.[†]

We were deeply interested in it, as much by the new light it threw upon the evolution of Russian music and its greatest adepts, as by the details it revealed respecting Borodin's double vocation; for he, like so many other Russian composers, combined an artistic life with a totally different order of professional duties.

We believe we are doing a useful work in making known the life of Borodin to those who have applauded his works. We have taken Monsieur Stassoff's biographical notice as a groundwork. To this we have added a few personal reminiscences, and some information from the correspondence which Borodin kept up with his Belgian friends,

[*] This notice, published in 1887 in *Le Messager Historique*, was republished in 1889, with a collection of 104 letters of Borodin and several articles of musical criticism, by Monsieur Souvorine, editor of the *Novoë Vremya*.

[†] Monsieur P. Tsitogtsian, now engineer at Alexandropol, Messieurs G. Mochekoff and A. Foniakoff. This last had been a pupil of Borodin's at St Petersburg.

especially with Monsieur G. Huberti, professor at the Conservatoire at Brussels; we have also supplied an analysis of Borodin's posthumous and crowning work, "Prince Igor," which was still unpublished when Monsieur Stassoff's book appeared. The latter collaborated with Borodin in the *mise en scène* of this opera. Above all, we have drawn largely from Borodin's correspondence, which, as a literary work, Monsieur Stassoff considers quite as remarkable as his musical compositions.

For some time Borodin found himself constantly in Liszt's society, and that portion of his correspondence in which he depicts Liszt in turn as virtuoso, professor, musical critic and autocrat of a little circle of pupils and *cognoscenti*, is not the least interesting, or the least instructive.

There exists, perhaps, no better portrait of the great Hungarian master.

In translating these private letters we seem irresistibly to recall the recollection of Borodin, and to hear him speak again with that dignity, simplicity and kindliness which never failed him, and which drew so many hearts towards him. We should feel glad if we succeeded in making those love the man who admired the musician; for we are convinced that the genius of the one was as great as the heart of the other.

I.

ALEXANDER BORODIN.

His Life and Works.

BORODIN AND LISZT

—o—

I.

A DOUBLE VOCATION.

ALEXANDER PORPHYRIEWITCH BORODIN was born at St Petersburg, October 31st, 1834. On his father's side he was descended from the Princes Imeretinsky, the last kings of Imeretia, the most beautiful of those ancient kingdoms of the Caucasus, where the flora of the East blossoms in the shadow of the eternal snows. The ancient kings of Imeretia are said to have claimed descent from David, and quartered in their arms the harp and the sling.

This legendary descent may be too remote and too obscure to have exercised any influence upon the genius of Borodin, but it is impossible to ignore the influence which produced in him a marked predilection for the rhythms and modes of the East, although it was never permitted him to gaze

A

upon its skies. Borodin inherited from his father the oriental type characteristic of the fine races of the Caucasus.

At the time of his birth, his father was sixty-two years of age, his mother twenty-five. Thus, heredity accounts also for the delicate constitution which did not allow the genius of Borodin to fulfil its early promise.

One circumstance which steadily interfered with the complete development of his artistic faculties was the twofold taste for music and science which manifested itself in him from his earliest years.

From the age of twelve, Borodin began to study science in company with young Schtchigleff, who afterwards devoted himself successfully to teaching music.

Schtchigleff was at this time a little prodigy, and in the interval between two lessons in chemistry the children, under the eyes of a somewhat second-rate German professor, would play the symphonies of Haydn, or Beethoven, and especially the works of Mendelssohn, arranged as pianoforte duets.

They attended concerts assiduously and were not slow to acquire a real passion for chamber-music. In order to devote themselves to it more completely, Borodin took lessons in the 'cello and flute, and Schtchigleff in the violin. Borodin's first composition, a concerto for flute and piano, written in 1847, at the age of thirteen, dates from this period. His second composition was a trio for two violins and violoncello, upon a theme from Robert Le Diable; a somewhat crude piece of work, but the instrumental portion of which was written *in parts*, without score, which already pointed to uncommon talents.

It soon became necessary to come to a decision with regard to the studies of young Borodin. The University of St Petersburg was at that time the scene of disturbances which induced his mother to let him pursue his studies at the Academy of Medicine and Surgery, where he was admitted in 1850, before he had attained his sixteenth year.

The family crossed the Neva to the district of Wybourg in order to be nearer to the Academy. Borodin set to work with ardour, and passed his examinations brilliantly. Unfortunately, religion formed part of the programme of higher education as it still does in Russia, and Borodin was sent down in consequence of an examination in which he cited, in language of too great freedom, a passage of Scripture. This was, however, his only reverse.

During his stay at the Academy of Medicine, he continued to study chemistry under Professor Zinine, whose laboratory he frequented from the third year of his academical course, despite the opposition of the professor, who thought it inconceivable that a student so backward in his studies could work there with any profit. Zinine soon changed his opinion and became one of the warmest patrons of the pupil who was ere long to succeed to his chair.

Meanwhile, music was not neglected; though Borodin spent the greater part of his time in the laboratory, he still cultivated his favourite art with the faithful Schtchigleff. No matter what the weather, our two friends took long journeys on foot, the one carrying his violin, the other his 'cello or flute, to take part in some musical gathering. Sometimes these were interminable. Schtchigleff remembers one that began at seven in the evening and lasted until the same hour next day.

The following anecdote is also borrowed from Schtchigleff's reminiscences :—

"One night the two friends were making their way home along a footpath, a few yards apart; it was pitch dark and the street lamps gave an uncertain light. Suddenly Schtchigleff heard a loud noise, succeeded by complete silence. He hastened to his friend's assistance, when he caught harmonious sounds proceeding from underground; he soon grasped what had happened. Borodin had fallen into a cellar, and his first care was to ascertain that his flute was none the worse."

These gatherings often took place at the house of an enthusiastic amateur, Monsieur Gawrouschkiewitch, attaché to the Imperial Chancery. Borodin would venture sometimes to take the part of second 'cello. This was his first school, and thirty years later he wrote a letter to Gawrouschkiewitch, in which we see that these first musical meetings still lived in his memory.

At this time Borodin was a great admirer of German music and, to use his own expression, "impregnated with Mendelssohnism." All his friends were German students, his mother preferring their society to that of the Russian students, whose way of life was distasteful to her.

The influence of nationality was, however, growing upon him, and at Gawrouschkiewitch's meetings he was already upholding Seroff * in his defence of Glinka against the German composers.

Borodin continued his essays in composition. He wrote "romances," as they are called in Russia, but was careful not to show them to anyone ; chamber-music was his chief preoccupation.

Once Gawrouschkiewitch tried to induce him to

* State councillor, composer and musical critic, born at St Petersburg in 1820. Author of several operas ; "Judith" (1863), "Rogneda" (1865), "La Force Maligne" (1871, a posthumous work). In Russia he has often been erroneously compared to Wagner, "whom he recalls by the same fundamental poverty of melodic invention," says Monsieur Cui in his *Music in Russia*. In spite of this unfortunate phrase, Monsieur Cui found himself subsequently compelled to proclaim the immense superiority of the Bayreuth Master as compared to Séroff.

write a quintet; he stoutly refused, alleging as an
excuse his work at the laboratory. " You know,"
he said, " with what mistrust artists receive the
music of amateurs. Besides, I should not dare to
face Zinine, who once said to me in public: ' Monsieur
Borodin, you would do well to occupy yourself less
with "romances." You know that I rely upon you
as my successor; but you think of nothing but
music; you make a mistake in hunting two hares
at once.' "

This admonition did not deter Borodin from working conscientiously at fugue. In this the fourth
year of his medical studies, he wrote a three-part
fugue, in the German style, but almost at the same
time he produced a scherzo in B minor for pianoforte, in which, for the first time in his compositions,
the national character seems to preponderate.

In 1856, Borodin was appointed surgeon to one
of the hospitals of the territorial army.

Here his sensibility underwent some rude shocks.
We are told that one of his first duties was the
treatment of some serfs to whom a colonel, their
proprietor, had applied the knout. It is true that
these particular serfs had, in the first instance,
knouted the colonel himself in revenge for his ill-
treatment. The spine of each of these poor
wretches presented one large sore, the bone was
exposed, and numerous splinters had to be extracted

from the lacerated flesh. Borodin fainted, unable to endure the sight.

His hospital work did not interfere, however, with his music. It was at this date that the national influence began to decidedly preponderate over the German. His meetings with Moussorgsky* were not unconnected with this psychological evolution.

Borodin himself shall tell the story of this acquaintance, extracted from the articles which he wrote upon Moussorgsky in 1881, shortly after that composer's death.

"I met Moussorgsky for the first time in the autumn of 1856. I had just been appointed army surgeon. Moussorgsky was an officer in the 'Preobajensky' † regiment. He was then seventeen. Our meeting took place at the hospital in which we were both serving ; we met in a common-room, which we both found equally dull. Both of us felt the same need for expansion, and we were not long in fraternising. The same evening we had an invitation to the house of the principal medical officer. Monsieur Popoff had a marriageable daughter, and

* Modeste Petrowitch Moussorgsky, born at Toropetz in 1839, one of the most distinguished musicians of the New Russian School, author of "Boris Godounoff," and of "Khovanschtchina," died March 28th, 1881.

† A celebrated body-guard regiment, founded by Peter the Great. [Translator.]

frequently invited the doctors and officers on
duty.

"Moussorgsky was what is popularly termed a
smart officer, elegant in dress and in person : small
feet, hair well trimmed, nails correct, aristrocratic
hands, distinguished in carriage and choice in conversation ; he spoke with some affectation and
sprinkled his discourse with French phrases a trifle
pretentiously. In all this there was a touch of
fatuity, but it was very slight and was tempered by
a really superior education. He was a favourite
with the ladies, and would sit down to the piano
and play with grace and expression fragments from
the 'Trovatore' or 'Traviata,' enchanted to hear his
feminine audience murmur his praises in chorus.

"I met Moussorgsky three or four times at Popoff's
and in the common-room of the hospital. Then I
lost sight of him. Popoff resigned, and there were
no more evening gatherings. As to myself, I gave
up my duties on being appointed assistant lecturer
in chemistry at the Academy of Medicine."

Borodin did not see Moussorgsky again until
1859.

"I met him once more," he writes, "at the house
of one of the assistant professors of the Academy,
Monsieur Ivanowsky, doctor to the School of
Artillery　Moussorgsky had then left the army.

"He was no longer the handsome youth that I

had known at Popoff's; he had grown stout and lost his fine bearing, but he was as careful as ever of his personal appearance. His habits were just the same and his foppishness had grown if anything a degree more marked. On being introduced, we had no difficulty in recognising each other.

" Moussorgsky assured me that he had only re-signed in order to devote himself to music. It was our chief topic of conversation. I was at that time enthusiastic over Mendelssohn; Schumann was unknown to me. Moussorgsky was already a frequent visitor to Balakireff's,* and his head was filled with a number of new works of which I had no idea.

" Ivanowsky asked us to play Mendelssohn's A minor symphony as a duet. Moussorgsky at first made some objections and begged to be excused the andante, which, he said, was not symphonic, and rather resembled one of the 'Songs without Words' orchestrated.

" He played the first movement and the scherzo. Moussorgsky afterwards began to speak with en-thusiasm of Schumann's symphonies. He played

* Mily Alexeiwitch Balakireff, born in 1836 at Nijni-Novgorod, exercised a weighty influence upon the New Russian School, as we shall see later on. Besides his orchestral works ("King Lear," "Thamara," Overtures, etc.) and compositions for piano ("Islamey"), he published, in 1866, a remarkable collection of national airs.

fragments of the one in E flat major. Suddenly
he broke off, saying:

"'Now for the mathematics!'

"All this was quite new to me and captivated me
from the first. Seeing that it took my fancy, he
played other new works, and I soon learned that he
was a composer himself, which increased the interest his personality had awakened in me. He
then played a scherzo of his own, and on reaching
the trio, he whispered to me:

"'This is quite Oriental.'

"I was astonished at these musical forms which
were quite novel to me. I cannot say they pleased
me at first. I was bewildered, but by dint of
listening I soon began to appreciate them and
find in them a certain charm. I must confess that
when Moussorgsky had told me of his intention
to devote himself seriously to music I took this
declaration at first for a bit of braggadocia and
laughed in my sleeve. But after hearing his
scherzo, I asked myself: 'Can I believe it or not?'"

In 1862 Borodin was introduced in his turn to
Balakireff's set. This brought about a third meeting with Moussorgsky.

"On my return from abroad, I made the acquaintance of Balakireff, and met Moussorgsky at
his house for the third time. We recognised each
other and recalled our first interviews.

" Moussorgsky had made great progress in composition.   Balakireff wished to make me acquainted with the music of his school, especially with a symphony by one of its members, Monsieur Rimsky-Korsakoff,* a naval officer who had just started on a long journey to North America.   Moussorgsky and Balakireff went to the piano, Moussorgsky taking the treble.   I was struck by the brilliance and depth, the power and beauty of this music. They played the finale of the symphony.   Moussorgsky soon found out that I too was a composer, and asked me to play him something.   I was much embarrassed and refused point blank "

Henceforward Balakireff, though two years his junior, became Borodin's real and only master, as he had been that of Cui, Moussorgsky and Rimsky-Korsakoff, teaching them the technique, the æsthetics, the instrumentation, and above all, the true spirit of a musical work.

Similar instruction was imparted four years later by Balakireff to Borodin, but the latter was better prepared for it.   Beethoven and Glinka were

* Nicholas Andreïewitch Rimsky-Korsakoff, born at Tickwin in 1844, served as naval officer until 1873.   He then became director of the Free School of Music founded by Balakireff in 1862.   He was the author of numerous symphonies and symphonic poems (" Antar," " Sadko," " La Grande Pâque Russe," " Scheherazade," etc.), and of several operas (" La Nuit de Mai," " La Pskovitaine," " Snegourotchka," " Mlada ").   He is considered by many people to be the head of the modern school since the death of Borodin.

familiar to him, besides which the Balakireff of 1862 was himself far superior to the Balakireff of 1858. He had produced, in the meantime, his best vocal compositions, and notably his score of " King Lear."

Balakireff's teaching was not subject to any authority; he dissected a work, and criticised it independently of all tradition.

Nothing further was required to drive the last traces of Mendelssohnism from Borodin's mind, but he is still more indebted to his master.

" Our relations," writes Balakireff to Monsieur Stassoff, " had important results for Borodin. He had so far considered himself an amateur, and did not attach much importance to his compositions; I was the first to reproach him with this indifference, and he immediately set to work with ardour to compose his symphony in E flat major."

Thus Borodin's artistic career dates from 1862. We shall return to him and to his fellow-workers in Balakireff's school, after sketching the principal features of his scientific career.

II.

In 1858 Borodin took the degree of Doctor of
Medicine, and in the following year he was sent
abroad to complete his scientific studies. He remained away three years and spent the greater
part of this time at Heidelberg, in Erlenmeyer's
laboratory, in company with a group of young
Russian scientists, among whom we must mention
the celebrated chemist Mendeleïeff. As soon as the
fine warm weather came, the young men started
with their knapsacks on their backs and travelled
for the greater part of the summer. Monsieur Mendeleïeff himself describes this nomadic existence.

" We started with light baggage, one knapsack
between two of us; we wore blouses and tried to
pass ourselves off as artists, which, in Italy, is
always advantageous to the traveller's purse. We
bought ourselves linen *en route*, and left it by way
of a tip to the waiters. Thus we visited Venice,
Verona and Milan in the spring of 1860, and

Genoa and Rome in the autumn of the same year."

Borodin afterwards spent a very short time in Paris.

"On our first trip we had an interesting adventure. Near Verona, our carriage was visited by the Austrian police in search of an Italian prisoner, condemned for political reasons, who had made his escape. Borodin's southern type attracted the attention of the police, who believed they had found in him the man they were seeking. They ransacked our slender baggage from top to bottom and questioned us ; but they soon found that we were peaceable Russian students and left us alone. Scarcely had we passed the Austrian frontier and entered the States of Sardinia, when our travelling companions began to make much of us, to embrace us, to cry 'Evviva' and to sing at the top of their voices. The prisoner was amongst us and yet had passed unobserved. Thanks to the suspicions aroused by Borodin's physiognony he had escaped from the clutches of Austria."

These journeys were an inexhaustible source of artistic enjoyment, even when music played but a small part in them. It was thanks to music, however, that Borodine made the acquaintance of his wife, Mademoiselle Catherine Sergeïewna Protopopowa. She was an excellent musician and initiated him into the styles of Schumann and Chopin.

One of Borodin's letters, a translation of which we print at the end of the first part of this book, gives us a glimpse of the love idyll of which Heidelberg was then the scene, and of which they were the hero and heroine.

During this period Borodin made but one essay in musical composition, a sextet in D major for strings, without double bass, which was performed at Heidelberg in 1860. This was still quite " Mendelssohnian." " I composed it to please the Germans," he wrote to Schtchigleff. After his return to Russia it was not heard of again.

In 1862 he was appointed assistant lecturer in chemistry at the Academy of Medicine. One of his pupils, Professor Dolroslawine, has devoted the following lines to the memory of his old teacher, whose colleague he afterwards became :—

" We were students in our second year when Borodin made his first appearance in the laboratory. He was a fine young man ; he was attired in a light summer overcoat and wore no official costume. He walked slowly and with a nonchalant air into the private room of Professor Zinine. The report soon spread that this young man was Borodin. All Zinine's students had heard of his expected return.

"Gifted with an expansive nature, Zinine was the friend of all his pupils, but he looked upon Borodin as an adopted son. For Borodin, Zinine was a true father. There were no scientific labours upon which they had not exchanged ideas.

"Almost to the day of his death, Borodin lived in an apartment on the same floor as his laboratory. He spent whole days there in the midst of his students. Possessed of a very even temper, he was always ready to break off his work to answer the questions of his pupils, who all felt quite at home with him.

"Borodin did not, however, forget his music; he was always humming as he worked, and often discussed with us the novelties of the hour, the various schools of music and the technicalities of modern compositions. We often heard the tones of his piano.

"Above all, it was his kindness that won our admiration. We could always approach him, display our ideas, give free rein to our thoughts without fear of being repulsed or of receiving an evasive answer. The only signs of impatience which he showed were provoked by our negligence or want of care.

"'Little father,' he would then say, 'if you continue to work in that style you will not be long in destroying our fine collection of instruments;'

or : ' How can you make such bad smells in such a beautiful laboratory ? ' And he would send the careless pupil to work in another room.

"His relations with the students did not stop at the threshold of the laboratory. Most of them were received into his house as friends. They constantly took their meals there when they worked over hours ; his house was always open to young people. Everyone could rely upon him, and it was often said that one could not meet Borodin without being solicited for a place for one or other of his old pupils."

Borodin lectured till his death. One year before this event his professorship was renewed for the last time for another five years, according to Russian law, which admits as the maximum thirty-five years of active teaching. He taught chiefly experimental chemistry, and had the control of the laboratory.

Towards the close of his studies, Borodin devoted himself to long experimental researches in chemistry. His works have been published in technical reviews both in Russia and abroad, notably in the *Journal of the Society of Chemistry and Physics*, the *Records of the Academy of Science*, the *Annals of Chemistry of Liebig*, the *Journal of Chemistry of Erlenmeyer*, etc.

According to an article by his successor and

former pupil, Professor Dianine, in the *Novoe Vremya* of February 19th, 1887, "Among the eight chemical treatises which he published in 1862, the 'Researches upon the Fluoride of Benzole' is the most remarkable. He also published, on his return to Russia, a work upon 'The Solidification of Aldehydes,' which attracted the attention of the scientific world. In his last years he was specially engaged in researches of great interest for physiology and medicine, on the transformation of azotic bodies, and invented a most convenient nitrometre for the volumetric determination of the azote in organic compositions. Borodin's method has come into general use in the laboratories of the Academy, and his process is described in all the text-books. He leaves twenty treatises upon chemistry, without including short notes."

On his return from the Antwerp Exhibition, where his artistic tastes had been gratified to the full, he was never tired of talking of the collection of instruments and chemical compounds which he had admired there, and the catalogues of which he had most carefully collected.

Besides teaching at the Academy of Medicine, Borodin also lectured in chemistry, in 1863, at the Academy of Forestry.

He was one of the most ardent advocates of the admission of women to the higher education, and founded, with Madame Taruowskaïa and Professor Rudnieff, the School of Medicine for Women at St Petersburg. He taught chemistry there from 1872, and interested himself warmly in this institution until his death.

His relations with the female students were not less cordial than with the young men of the Academy, and his old pupils decorated his coffin with a silver crown bearing this inscription :—" To the founder, protector and defender of the School of Medicine for Women, to the supporter and friend of the students. From the women doctors qualified between 1872 and 1887."

I I I.

LET us resume the history of Borodin's artistic career where we left off—that is to say, at the moment when, acting on the advice of Balakireff, he began to compose his first symphony in E flat major.

This work, begun in 1862, was not finished till 1867. During this period, the genius of Borodin was completely transformed under the influence of Balakireff and of the concerts of the Free School of Music. As Monsieur Stassoff remarks, Balakireff, Moussorgsky and Rimsky-Korsakoff were better prepared than Borodin to reflect the national influence; like Glinka, they had spent their youth in villages, in the heart of Russia, while Borodin had hardly ever left the capital. Still, the national character makes itself clearly felt in this first symphony, especially in the trio of the scherzo and in the adagio.

Balakireff, who was then conductor of the concerts of the Russian Musical Society, had Borodin's first symphony performed on January 4th, 1869, in the Salle de la Noblesse. The directors of the society had appealed to young composers, and a number of *dilettanti* had presented themselves, among whom Borodin was nearly lost sight of. After a first rehearsal, the general impression was bad, and the symphony, the band parts of which were certainly very imperfect, was declared to be full of difficulties and daring flights. After subsequent rehearsals, however, opinion began to change. On the day of performance success was not long in being assured; the first movement met with scanty applause, but the scherzo, briskly carried through by Balakireff, awoke a storm of applause; it was encored and the composer was called for. After the finale Borodin was recalled several times.

Dargomijsky* had just written his " Convive de pierre," a work of genius unequalled, as regards lyric declamation, among the dramatic compositions of the New Russian School. He was then on his death-bed, and being unable to hear this symphony, on the success of which he had built such great hopes, he was anxiously awaiting a visit from

* Alexander Sergeïevitch Dargomijsky, born February 2d, 1813, was the composer of several operas—" Esmeralda," " La Triomphe de Bacchus," " La Roussalka," and lastly, " Le Convive de pierre,' a posthumous work, the libretto by Pushkin, one of the masterpieces of Russian opera.

Borodin, to learn from his lips the result of an attempt which he looked upon as one of the most important battles yet fought by the New School. He never heard of Borodin's success ; Dargomijsky died the following day, January 5th, 1869, at five in the morning.

The success of this first symphony had a decisive influence upon Borodin's artistic career.

The critics, however, were unfavourable, and Séroff himself ventured to write the following lines in the *Golos :*—" The symphony *by somebody of the name of Borodin* pleased very few hearers, and only the friends of the composer applauded and recalled him with enthusiasm."

On the other hand, here is the opinion of a master whose judgment will not be challenged. On September 3d, 1880, Liszt wrote to Borodin :—

" I am very remiss in telling you what you know better than I do, that the instrumentation of your renowned symphony in E flat major is written by a master hand and accords perfectly with the composition. It was a keen enjoyment to me to hear it at the rehearsals and at the concert at Baden-Baden. The best connoisseurs, as well as a very numerous public, applauded you heartily."

After this work, which would be sufficient of itself to class Borodin among the greatest musicians of our time, he occupied himself especially with

vocal compositions. In this he obeyed the same
impulse as his friends.

Cui was writing "William Ratcliff"; Moussorgsky, "Boris Godounoff"; Rimsky-Korsakoff,
"La Pskovitaine." Balakireff himself, who was
not however much inclined by disposition towards
dramatic music, began at this time to compose
"L'oiseau D'or." Borodin set to work to write an
opera, taking for his libretto a drama by Mey—"La
Fiancée du Czar"; but he soon tired of his subject
and abandoned his work when already far advanced. From this period (1867-1870) date his
incomparable songs (romances), an unbroken series
of masterpieces of passionate and expressive declamation.

In 1867 he composed "La Princesse Eudormie"
(The Sleeping Beauty); in 1868 "Vieille Chanson,"
or "Chanson de la Forêt Sombre" (Song of the
Gloomy Forest); then "Dissonance," "La Reine des
Mers" (The Sea Queen), "Mon Chant est Amer"*
(My Song is bitter); and finally, in 1870, "La Mer"
(The Sea), that touching ballad which, among all
these works of art, undoubtedly takes the first
place.

A talented singer, Madame Molas, a pupil of
Dargomijsky, who was in Borodin's set, knew how

* An English Version of this Song is published by Messrs
Stanley, Lucas & Weber, London. (Translator.)

to do justice to these vocal compositions.   Borodin
declared that in certain of his melodies, "Mon
Chant est Amer" among others, the task of the
interpreter was at least equal to that of the composer in the creation of the work.

   These compositions, now translated and published
in several editions, have passed out of the range of
criticism.   Let us see how they were then reviewed
by Monsieur Laroche, one of the most weighty
critics in St Petersburg.

   Speaking of "La Princesse Endormie," Monsieur
Laroche wrote in 1874 in the *Golos :*—" The greater
part of this romance is written pianissimo.   No doubt
the composer uses this mode of expression wisely out
of consideration for his audience, or it may be from
a sense of shame, as things are whispered which
one would not dare to say aloud.   And certainly
in all his works he seems to be bent on giving
his hearers some disagreeable sensation.   The title
of one of his songs, " Dissonance," appears to be his
motto.   He must always introduce a dissonance
somewhere, often a number of them, and occasionally, as in this song, nothing but dissonance.
Once only, in his quartet, he seems to have abjured
his ideal.   Reflecting on the abundance of his
cacophonies, he wrote one day in self-defence, " Mon
Chant est Amer ; " but this good inspiration passed
away too soon and ended in nothing, for last

autumn he published, through Bessel, three new romances which are steeped with the old poison. It is hard to believe, but none the less indisputable, that this bitter enemy of music is not without talent; for side by side with the unwholesome and misshapen extravagances with which his work abounds, we occasionally find rich harmonies. After all, it may be that the impulse which inclines him towards what is unlovely is contrary to his native instinct, and is only the bitter fruit of a defective education in art."

Posterity has avenged Borodin upon such criticisms, clever, perhaps, but inept.

I V.

BORODIN'S letters show us in their true light the features of Balakireff and his school, which had so great an influence on the destinies of Russian art. It is especially in his letters to Madame Karmalina, Glinka's niece, that we find the story of that mutual instruction which, for the majority of Russian musicians of our time, took the place of academical training.

On April 15th, 1875, he wrote:—" Cui is working hard at ' Angelo ' (Thisbe) ; Modeste (Moussorgsky) is writing 'Khovanschtchina'; Rimsky-Korsakoff is working for the Free School ; he writes counterpoint and teaches his pupils all kinds of musical devices. He is writing a monumental course of instrumentation which will be without a rival in the world; but he also has no leisure, and for the moment has abandoned his work.

" You have doubtless heard of the disruption of

our school. It is not astonishing. It is in the natural order of things. So long as we were eggs laid by one hen (and that hen Balakireff), we were all more or less alike; but when the young chickens came out of their shells, each one clothed himself in different feathers, and when our wings had grown, each one flew away in a different direction.

" This want of similarity in the tendency and character of our work is not, to my mind, the saddest side of the business. It was inevitable as soon as our artistic individuality had matured; Balakireff did not understand this and has not grasped it even yet.

" Many people have been distressed to see Korsakoff take a retrograde step and give himself up to the study of musical archæology. For myself I can quite understand it, and it does not trouble me. Korsakoff's development was the reverse of mine. While I began with the classics, Korsakoff began with Glinka, Liszt and Berlioz. When he had steeped himself in these he moved into an unknown sphere, which had for him an entirely novel character."

In a letter of June 1st, 1876, he again refers to the break-up of Balakireff's school :—"We do not agree upon the word disruption. You yourself find great dissimilarity between us, and you say that

each one's work differs entirely from that of
another in character, inspiration, etc.   But it is just
in this that disruption lies.   It is clear that there
are no rivalries or personal questions between us;
nor could there be on account of the respect we
have for each other.   It is thus in every branch of
human activity; in proportion to its development,
individuality triumphs over the schools, over that
heritage which men have gathered from their
masters.   A hen's eggs are all alike, the chickens
differ somewhat, and in time cease to resemble
each other at all.   One becomes a dark-plumed
fighting cock, another a white and peaceful hen.
It is the same with us.   We have all derived from
the set in which we have lived the common
characteristics of genius and species; but each of
us, like an adult cock or hen, bears his own
character and individuality.   If, on this account,
we are thought to have separated from Balakireff,
fortunately, it is not so; we are as fond of him as
ever, and spare nothing to keep up the same relations with him as before.   He has set himself to
complete ' Thamara,' God willing !

   "As to us, we continue to interest ourselves in
each other's musical productions.   If we are not
always pleased, that is quite natural, tastes differ ;
and even in the same person tastes vary with age.
It could not be otherwise."

On January 19th, 1877, he writes :—" Here is a very pleasant and gratifying piece of news of which you doubtless are ignorant. Balakireff, the amiable Balakireff, has come to life again as regards music. He has always been the same Mily Alexeïewitch, ardent defender of the sharps and flats and all the minutest details of some composition which formerly he would not hear mentioned. Now he besieges Korsakoff once more with his letters about the Free School, takes the liveliest interest in the composition of concert programmes, works at his 'Thamara,' and is finishing an arrangement, for four hands, of Berlioz's ' Harolde en Italie,' commissioned by a Paris publisher. In short, he is resuscitated."

About this time Borodin collaborated with his friends, Rimsky-Korsakoff, Liadoff and Cui, in a work, apparently humorous, but really of a serious nature, entitled " Paraphrases," twenty-four variations, and fourteen little pieces for piano, on a favourite theme obligato, " dedicated to little pianists who can play the air with one finger of each hand."

This theme, consisting of four bars, must be played by the first performer on the upper octaves of the piano, while the second player performs the paraphrases, for which more than a mere tyro is needed.

For this lengthy work Borodin wrote three pieces, by no means the least interesting, entitled "Polka," "Marche Funèbre" and "Requiem"; this last, in which a liturgical chant is developed as a fugue upon the popular and persistent air, is especially striking.

In one of his last letters addressed to his friends, Monsieur and Madame G. Huberti, December 14th, 1886, Borodin relates the origin of this work :—

"I take the liberty of sending you, for your little girls, my—or rather *our*—'Paraphrases,' twenty-four variations, and fourteen little pieces for piano on the favourite theme of the Coteletten Polka:

 etc.

which is so popular with the little ones in Russia. It is played with the first finger of each hand. The origin of this humorous work is very funny. One day Gania (one of my adopted daughters) asked me to play a duet with her.

" 'Well, but you do not know how to play, my child.'

" 'Yes, indeed, I can play this :—

 etc.'

"I had to yield to the child's request, and so I improvised the polka which you will find in the collection. The four keys, C major, G major, F minor and A minor, of the four parts of the polka, in which the unchanging theme of the Coteletten Polka makes a kind of canto fermo or counter-point, caused much laughter among my friends, afterwards joint-authors of the 'Paraphrases.' They were amused. First one and then another wanted to try his hand at a piece in this style. The joke was well received by our friends. We amused ourselves by performing these things with people who could not play the piano. Finally, we were requested to publish this work. Rahter became the proprietor and publisher. This music fell into Liszt's hands, who was delighted with it. He wrote a charming letter about it to one of his friends in St Petersburg ; the letter was very flattering to the author of the 'Paraphrases.' One day the friend of Liszt's who had received this letter mentioned it in a musical article. The critics, our enemies, were infuriated, and said that Liszt could not have approved of such a work, that he never wrote the letter, that the whole thing was a falsehood, and finally that we composers had compromised ourselves by the publication of such a work.

"When Liszt heard all this he laughed heartily. He wrote to us :—'If this work is considered *compromising*, let me *compromise* myself with you.' It was then that he sent the scrap of music that serves as an introduction to my Polka, requesting Rahter to print it in the second edition of the 'Paraphrases' already in the press. In view of Liszt's great authority, Rahter thought well to engrave the fac-simile of the leaflet sent by the great master. The reproduction of this leaflet was printed and added to the music of the first edition. Our enemies were silenced. Liszt was very fond of this humorous work, and it always amused him to play it with his pupils."

The page added by Liszt bore the title:—" Variation for the second edition of the *marvellous* work of Borodin, Cesar Cui, Liadoff and Rimsky-Korsakoff, by their devoted Franz Liszt, Weimar, July 28th, 1880. To be placed between pages 9 and 10 of the early edition, after the finale of C. Cui, and as prelude to the polka by Borodin."

The personality of Balakireff reappears in one of Borodin's letters to Monsieur Stassoff, July 23d 1880:—" You will remember that at Balakireff's request I had my first symphony sent back from abroad. As soon as it had arrived, Balakireff ceased to speak of it, and in fact he had no need for it. Having received a request from the Allgemeiner Musikverein, I once more returned my symphony to Baden-Baden, where it was performed on the 20th of June 1880 with great success, of which Monsieur C. Riedel, president of the Allgemeiner Musikverein, hastened to inform me the next day in a letter directed to 'Monsieur A. Borodin, composer, St Petersburg,' without any further address.

"I wrote immediately to Balakireff. He came at once, radiant, to congratulate me on my success. It was nine years since Balakireff had set foot inside my house. But his manner was just the same as if he had only left us the day before. He went to the piano as usual, played a quantity of good things, and only left us at midnight, after inquiring when we were going away. As we were staying a few days longer in St Petersburg, he promised to come and see us again.

"The next day he reappeared, gay and radiant, carrying under his arm a parcel of music for four hands, because, as he said, he wanted to play with Katia (Madame Borodin) Grieg's Dances, the symphonies of Svendson, etc. He played the piano, chatted, discussed, gesticulated with the greatest animation, and was glad to hear that we were not leaving for some days, or he would have been obliged to be separated from us for nearly three months. Naturally he let us hear 'Thamara,' etc.

"Two days later he came again with his music and pressed Katia to go to the piano without loss of time, just as if there had never been a nine years' interval in his visits."

V.

DRAMATIC WORKS—PRINCE IGOR—MLADA.

IN search of a libretto for an opera, Borodin addressed himself to Monsieur Stassoff. The latter furnished him with the plot of a libretto taken from a national epic poem, "The Epic of the Army of Prince Igor," which tells of an expedition of Russian princes against the Polovtsi, a nomadic people of the same origin as the ancient Turks, which had invaded the Russian principalities about the twelfth century. This poem, the author of which is unknown, is considered worthy to rank with the finest works of classic antiquity.*

The conflict between Russian and Asiatic nationalities, which forms the basis of the poem, must have attracted Borodin. He set to work with ardour, and began to prepare himself for the task of writing the poem of his opera by reading everything that could bear upon the subject.

---

* A German translation by Monsieur Cederholm was published at Moscow in 1825.

The methods of the scientist appear in the manner in which he undertook his task. He strove to impregnate himself with the atmosphere, and even with the language of the twelfth century, by searching the public libraries and deciphering the old epic poems—" The Battle of the Don," " The Battle of Mamai." He assimilated the epics and songs of the tribes who, like the Polovtsi, dwell in the steppes of Lesser Russia. He collected original melodies, and even had recourse to the celebrated traveller, Monsieur Hunfalvi, who transmitted to him the songs of Central Asia.

Remodelling Monsieur Stassoff's plot, he introduced, after Shakespeare's manner, comic characters to create artistic contrasts. Finally he began to compose some parts of the music, but at the end of a year he became the victim of a profound depression which none of his friends succeeded in overcoming. Monsieur Stassoff suggests that it was due to the influence of his connections, especially of his wife.

" The day had gone by," they told him, " to write operas on heroic or mythical subjects ; now-a-days one must treat the modern drama."

Borodin was inflexible, and when people deplored the loss of such accumulated materials, he invariably answered that these materials would go into his second symphony. He began to work hard at this, and the first allegro was written by the close of the autumn of 1871.

At this time the director of the Russian Opera, Monsieur Ghedeunoff, himself a distinguished dramatic author, proposed to mount a kind of opera-ballet entitled " Mlada," which was to include a fairy scene. The music of the ballet proper (as distinguished from the opera-ballet) was to be written by Minkus, the composer of " La Source," and Mousieur Stassoff was commissioned to invite the four champions of the Modern School, Borodin, Cui, Moussorgsky and Rimsky-Korsakoff to undertake the vocal part.

Our quartet assented and set to work with enthusiasm. The subject of " Mlada " recalled a period anterior to the introduction of Christianity into the Slavonic countries, and brought upon the stage the customs of the ancient Slavs of the Baltic.

Nothing further was needed to inspire Borodin, who undertook the fourth act. This act in particular included religious scenes, the apparition of the ghosts of the old Slavonic princes, the deluge and destruction of the temple. In the midst of this magnificent setting, human passion found expression in a grand scene between Jaromir and Voïslawa, the principal personages of the drama.

Faithful to his methods, Borodin began to study the customs and religion of these tribes. He read and re-read the work of Professor Srezniewski on the religious ceremonies of the Slavonic races, and soon created a series of scenes, of which the inspiration equalled the colouring.

This was early in 1872. He was ill about this time and had to keep to his room for a fortnight; during this period he scarcely left the piano. Those who went to see him invariably found him composing, his eyes ablaze with inspiration. All his friends acknowledged the crushing superiority of those pages of " Mlada " which came from his pen.

Yet the enterprise of Monsieur Ghedeunoff failed. The scenery was ready, the costumes designed from authentic documents, the *corps de ballet* were rehearsing the fantastic flights of the " roussalki," (Russian water nymphs) suspended and cradled among the branches. But the mounting that was contemplated involved the most extravagant expenditure. All was laid aside ; the composers replaced their compositions in their portfolios, and Borodin returned to his second symphony.*

" Prince Igor," however, was not forgotten, and an opportunity was only required to revive in Borodin all the enthusiasm with which the subject had inspired him a few years before.

---

* The finale of " Mlada," by Borodin, has recently been published, by Monsieur Belaïeff of Leipzig.

This opportunity occurred in the winter of 1874. He then received a visit from one of his favourite pupils, Dr Schonoroff, who had left St Petersburg at the conclusion of his studies to enter the service of the Government of the Caucasus. They had never met since, and Borodin hastened to tell his young friend about his scientific and artistic labours. He spoke to him naturally of " Prince Igor" and the neglect which had befallen the half-written score. Monsieur Schonoroff had not much difficulty in proving to him that this desertion was a crime, and that no subject could be better adapted to the genius of its composer.

The next day Borodin hastened in radiant spirits to the Imperial Library to announce to Monsieur Stassoff that "Igor" was resuscitated and was about to enter on a new existence. Borodin re-wrote his libretto in order to introduce a portion of the materials collected for " Mlada." *

* The entire libretto of " Mlada" has been more recently set to music by Monsieur Rimsky-Korsakoff, and was performed in St Petersburg in 1892, when it met with considerable success.

VI.

IT is time to give some information about the libretto of " Prince Igor." This opera was published after Borodin's death by the exertions of his friends, especially Rimsky-Korsakoff and Glaz-ounoff, who completed and orchestrated the unfinished portions. The libretto is certainly far from satisfying our Western ideas of a good dramatic work, but it may be suited to win a great success in Russia, since it touches the chord of national sentiment.

Moreover, the libretto is not worse than that of many Russian operas, beginning with " La vie pour le Czar," the most popular of them all, which owes its lasting success as much to the patriotic scenes it displays as to the music of Glinka.

We will follow the libretto of " Prince Igor " step by step through the French version which accompanied the score published by Monsieur Belaïeff of Leipzig. The prologue takes place in the marketplace of the town of Poutivle, the residence of Igor, Prince of Séwersk. The Prince and his army are prepared to start in pursuit of the Polovtsi, who have been already conquered by Swiatoslaw, Prince of Kiev.

Igor has taken no part in this victory, and desires to fight the Polovtsi in the plains of the Don, where they have taken refuge : " I would fain break my lance in their remotest deserts ; there I will leave my ashes, or, dipping my helmet in the Don, I will slake my thirst in its waters." *

An eclipse of the sun darkens the sky. At this fatal presage the people implore Igor not to set forth. But the Prince is resolute ; he takes his son Wladimir, after having confided his wife, Princess Jaroslawna, to the care of his brother-in-law, Prince Galitzky, who remains within the walls of Poutivle.

The first scene of the first act depicts the situation of the town after the departure of Igor. Prince Galitzky, a powerful and dissolute noble, seeks to win over the populace by means of festivities and amusements. He conspires against Igor with two deserters from the army, Eroschka and Skoula, musicians, players of the *goudok*, who sell their

---

* This quotation, as well as those that follow, is taken from the analysis of " The Epic of the Army of Igor," published in *Karamsin : History of Russia*, translated by St Thomas and Jauffret. Paris, 1819.

souls to the Prince. They are the two comic characters of the drama.

The second scene shows us Princess Jaroslawna bewailing the absence of her husband. There is no news from Igor and the Princess is uneasy at the intrigues of Prince Galitzky. Some young girls come to complain of the abduction of one of their companions, and after a violent scene the Princess drives Prince Galitzky from her apartments at the very moment when the boyards come to announce the defeat of the army of Igor on the Kayala. "At the third dawn," says the poem, "the Russian flags fell before the enemy, for no blood was left to be shed." Igor is wounded and taken prisoner together with Wladimir, and the Polovtsi are marching upon Poutivle.

Suddenly the alarm is sounded, cries resound, the glow of fire lights up the scene, the Polovtsi are attacking the town. The boyards draw their swords and swear to defend the Princess.

The second and third acts take place in the camp of the enemy.

The fair Kontschakowna, daughter of Khan Kontschak, appears surrounded by her companions. "On the shores of the azure sea," says the poem, "is heard the song of the Polovtsian maidens, and the ring of the gold carried off from the Russians."

It is the close of day. The Princess awaits the

arrival of Wladimir, son of Igor, who is enamoured
of her beauty. Night draws on, the Princess and
her women retire to their tents, and young
Wladimir sings a serenade before that of the
Princess, who hastens out to meet her love.

Their duet is interrupted by the arrival of Prince
Igor, who, weighed down by a great grief, is
wandering through the camp.

He is thinking of the inauspicious omen that
clouded the departure of his army. In vain he
seeks repose. His former glory is tarnished by
the shame of his captivity; his people will all
curse him, save Jaroslawna, his tender dove, who
will pardon him and share his sufferings.

While he is plunged in gloomy thought a guard
approaches him furtively. It is Ovlour, a Polowetz
converted to Christianity, who proposes to Igor to
prepare for flight; but to flee is unworthy of a
prince and Igor refuses.

Meanwhile day breaks; the Khan Kontschak
approaches his prisoner and pays homage to his
valour. The chronicle relates that Kontschak had
actually given Prince Igor attendants and a priest,
and permitted him to hunt at large with falcons.

He desires to show his friendliness by treating
him as a guest, and invites him to a feast which
serves as a pretext for a grand display of dances,
choruses and scenic effects.

The third act opens with the return of Khan Gsak, conqueror of Poutivle. The town has fallen into his power. He drags in his train booty and prisoners. This blow is too great; at the entreaties of his son, Wladimir, who places the honour of his country before his love, Igor at last consents to flee. Ovlour will have the horses in readiness, and give the signal of escape as soon as the camp is hushed in sleep.

Meanwhile, the Polovtsian warriors divide the spoil. Ovlour plies them with koumiss, and they soon fall into the sleep of drunkenness.

But Princess Kontschakowna has learned all; she visits the tent of Wladimir, calls him forth, and implores him not to leave her. He is on the point of yielding when Prince Igor appears.

Here follows the most dramatic scene in the work.

The presence of his father recalls Wladimir to a sense of duty, and the breathless supplications of the Princess are powerless against the stern inflexibility of the two Russian princes. In the midst of this conflict are heard the repeated calls of Ovlour.

The Princess, seeing herself conquered, gives a signal, clings to Wladimir and holds him back, while Igor escapes.

The Polovtsi hasten from all sides, seize Wladimir, and threaten him with death, in spite of the entreaties of Kontschakowna.

"If the old falcon has flown back to his nest," they say, "the young falcon will soon follow." Kontschak replies: "For that reason you must chain the young falcon by giving him a mate. He shall be the husband of Kontschakowna."

The fourth act takes the spectators back to Poutivle. Princess Jaroslawna is weeping on the terrace of her ruined palace, and contemplating the distant plain ravaged by the hostile army.

"O cruel winds, why did you lend your airy wings to the darts hurled against the warriors of my love? Was it not enough to move the waters of the azure sea, and to rock the ships of Russia upon its waves? O majestic Dnieper! thou hast pierced through awful rocks to rush through the country of the Polovtsi; thou hast borne on thy waters the boats of Swiatoslaw unto the camp of Kobiak. Bring me back the beloved of my heart, then I shall no longer daily charge the sea to bear to him the tribute of my tears. Brilliant star of day! thou pourest upon all mortals thy mild warmth and thy majestic glow, and yet thy ardent rays have consumed in the desert the armies of my well-beloved."

Two horsemen now draw near. They are Igor and Ovlour, who return after an adventurous journey of eleven days.

Igor is soon in the arms of Jaroslawna.

Igor and the Princess re-enter the Kremlin of Poutivle at the same moment when Eroschka and Skoula, the two deserters, come upon the scene. They see Igor and the Princess. If the Prince recognises them they are lost. To get out of the difficulty they can think of no better expedient than to sound the alarm and make themselves the bearer of the glad tidings of Igor's return. The people hasten to acclaim their Prince, who appears on the threshold of the Kremlin with Jaroslawna and the boyards.

Such is the libretto, to the *naïveté* of which we might often take exception if we did not know that it closely follows an heroic poem of which Borodin has faithfully preserved the situations, adding only so much as was necessary to graft the picturesque element on to the drama.

VII.

THE SCORE OF PRINCE IGOR.   SECOND SYMPHONY.

IT is through Borodin's correspondence that we learn best to appreciate the unending difficulties arising out of his double vocation, which never ceased to interfere with the completion of his favourite work.

He thus expresses himself in a letter of April 15th, 1875, addressed to a friend, Madame Ludmilla Ivanowna Karmalina, who seems to have been the confidant of his ambitions and his disappointments :—

"Every man is more or less of an egoist and likes to talk of himself. I am a man, and therefore not exempt from this failing ; so I will begin by telling you about myself. Since my last letter, I have lived in all manner of ways—rather ill than well. In consequence of the resignation of one of our professors of chemistry, I have been obliged to take over part of his lectures. This work required a lengthy preparation, and took up much of my time. Besides, our Academy is on its trial, and awaits the verdict of its judges. The situation is accidental, but it exercises a very bad influence upon the entire Academy, and consequently upon my particular chair. This gives me a great deal to do, and leads to my being taken up with a number of things useful, indispensable, or sometimes even useless. Add to this the troubles of slow promotion and financial embarrassment. All this is not conducive to cheerfulness, and leaves me but little time for my favourite occupations.

"Neither is my home very bright. My poor wife is always ill; this year she suffers more than usual. I busy myself a great deal with the education of women, in which I find a congenial exercise for my moral sympathies.

"In the midst of my academical and scientific work, commissions, committees and various meetings, I have very little time left to devote to music. Sometimes I can spare a moment to keep myself up with current events, to hear the compositions of my friends, etc. But even if actual time were not wanting, I have absolutely no mental leisure; tranquillity is indispensable to this, and my thoughts are elsewhere.

"I have indeed just completed a pianoforte arrangement of my first symphony, and that is all. The arrangement of the second is half-finished.

"Meanwhile, I am like a consumptive who, scarcely able to breathe, still dreams of a goat's-milk cure, of a journey to the south, of rambles through meadows carpeted with flowers. I, too, dream of writing an opera.

"But what a difference between the consumptive patient and myself! He might carry out his aspirations if health were restored to him, while I can hope for nothing better than to fall ill. In fact, when I am tied to the house with some indisposition, unable to devote myself to my ordinary work, when my head is splitting, my eyes running, and I have to blow my nose every minute, then I give myself up to composing.

"I have been thus indisposed twice this winter, and each time I have raised a new stone in my edifice.

"This edifice is 'Prince Igor.'

"I have already written a grand Polovtsian march, an air for Jaroslawna, the complaint of Jaroslawna in the last act, a short chorus for women in the camp of the Polovtsi, and Oriental dances, for the Polovtsi were an eastern people. I have collected a quantity of materials, and completed several numbers. But when shall I have finished? I know not. My only hope is in the summer; but in summer I ought to complete the orchestration of my second symphony, promised long ago, and to my shame never finished.

"I ought also to finish the piano arrangement for which Bessel* has long been waiting. To the great displeasure of Stassoff and Modeste Moussorgsky, I have sketched out a quartet for strings which I have not found time to finish either. It is shameful, piteous, ridiculous, but what can be done? Like Claud Frollo, there is nothing for me but to inscribe the word 'fatality' in Greek characters upon the wall and to possess myself in patience."

In another letter to the same lady, dated June 10th, 1876:—

"If I did not at once reply to your kind and affectionate letter, it was because it reached me at a moment of feverish academical activity. At the close of the year I am so hindered by commissions, boards of examination, theses, accounts and laboratory work, that I become positively incapable of writing a letter to a friend. I then resemble that character in one of Shakespeare's historical plays † who replies to every question: 'Anon, anon, sir!' During this time I am the most unmusical of men, and cease to remember that I ever occupied myself with music. As your letter speaks chiefly of this

* Publisher of Borodin's first works in St Petersburg.
† Henry IV.

art, I have put off answering it until the beginning
of the holidays. . . . You ask for news of ' Igor.'
When I speak of this work, I cannot help laughing
at myself.   It always reminds me of the magician
Finn in ' Russlane,' who is burning with love for
Naina, but forgets how time is flying and cannot
bring himself to decide his fate until both he and
his betrothed have grown grey with age.   I am
like him in attempting to compose an heroic opera
while time flies with the rapidity of an express
train.   Days, weeks, months, whole winters pass,
without my being able to set to work seriously.   It
is not that I could not find a couple of hours a day ;
it is that I have not leisure of mind to withdraw
myself from occupations and preoccupations which
have nothing in common with music.

"One needs time to concentrate oneself, to get
into the right key, otherwise the creation of a
sustained work is impossible.   For this I have only
a part of summer at my disposal.   In the winter I
can only compose when I am ill and have to give
up my lectures and my laboratory.

"So, my friends, reversing the usual custom, never
say to me, ' I hope you are well,' but, ' I hope you
are ill.'   At Christmas I had influenza and could
not go to the laboratory.   I stayed at home and
wrote the Thanksgiving Chorus in the last act
of ' Igor.'

"In summer I compose more, because I write in the best of health.

"I have written in all one act and a half out of four. I am satisfied with what I have done, as are also my friends. The Thanksgiving Chorus, performed by the orchestra of the Free School, obtained a great success, and it is a significant omen for the rest of my work.

"As a composer seeking to remain anonymous, I am shy of confessing my musical activity. This is intelligible enough. For others it is their chief business, the occupation and aim of life. For me, it is a relaxation, a pastime which distracts me from my principle business, my professorship. I do not follow Cui's example. I love my profession and my science. I love the Academy and my pupils. My teaching is of a practical character, and for this very reason takes up much of my time. I have to be constantly in touch with my pupils, male and female, because to direct the work of young people one must be always close to them. I have the interests of the Academy at heart. If, on the one hand, I want to finish my work, on the other hand I am afraid of devoting myself to it too assiduously and throwing any scientific work into the shade.

"But now, since the performance of the chorus from 'Igor,' the public know that I am composing an opera. There is no longer anything to conceal or be ashamed of. I am in the situation of a girl who has lost her innocence, and by that very fact has acquired a certain sort of liberty; now, *willy nilly*, I must finish the work.

" The good wishes of my friends and of the entire opera company will have their influence.

" I must observe, however, that from the dramatic point of view I have always been unlike the majority. Recitative does not enter into my nature or disposition. Although, according to some critics, I do not handle it altogether badly, I am far more attracted to melody and cantilena. I am more and more drawn to definite and concrete forms.

"In opera, as in decorative art, details and minutiæ are out of place. Bold outlines only are necessary; all should be clear and straightforward and fit for practical performances from the vocal and instrumental standpoint. The voices should occupy the first place, the orchestra the second.

"I am no judge of the way in which I shall succeed, but my opera will be nearer akin to ' Russlane ' than to ' The Stone Guest.' That I can vouch for.

"It is curious to see how all the members of our set agree in their praise of my work. While controversy rages amongst us on every other subject, all, so far, are pleased with ' Igor.' Moussorgsky,

the ultra realist, the innovating lyrico-dramatist
Cui, our master, Balakireff, so severe as regards
form and tradition, Wladimir Stassoff himself, our
valiant champion of everything that bears the
stamp of novelty or greatness.

"Such is the history of my natural child 'Igor,'
whose time has not yet come. From this unlawful
offspring I pass on to my lawful wife. Catherine
Sergeiewna thanks you for the kind messages you
sent, and sends her kind regards to you and your
husband; she was unable to see you because she
was ill. As a rule, her health is very bad, which
saddens our home, so charming in every other respect."

Again, on January 19th, 1877, he writes to the
same lady :—

"You and your husband have the gift of attach-
ing young hearts to yourselves. You have many
friends among our young university students of
both sexes from the Caucasus.* It could not be
otherwise, for youth must appreciate at a glance
your genuine kindness and unreserved warmth of
heart. But from the young let us pass to the old.
We, old sinners, are carried away as ever in the
vortex of life, of our profession, of study, science
and art. We are always hurrying on, never arriv-

* Madame Karmalina's husband was at that time military
governor of one of the provinces of the Caucasus.

ing anywhere. Time flies like an engine at full steam. Meanwhile, our beards grow grey, the wrinkles begin to show. We begin a hundred different things. Shall we ever succeed in finishing one or two? At heart I am always a poet. I cherish the hope of carrying through my opera to the last bar, but I often laugh at myself. I get on slowly and at long intervals. During the summer I worked but little.

"I am astonished that the greater part of 'Igor' should satisfy two such opposite schools of music. But most of my friends give the preference to the concerted pieces and the choruses. What will come of it? I have no idea. I should like to finish it for next season, but I am doubtful if I can do so.

"I have already written a great deal, but I have still materials in my portfolio. It all needs arranging, an enormous task, especially as regards those concerted and choral scenes that require large vocal and instrumental masses.

"I have just had a fresh disaster. The Musical Society had decided to perform my second symphony at one of their concerts. I was in the country and knew nothing of this decision. On arriving at St Petersburg I could not find the first part and the finale. The score of these two movements was lost. I searched in vain, it was not to be found; meanwhile, the Musical Society were demanding it, and there was no time to copy out the parts. What was to be done?

"As a climax to my bad luck I fell ill. It was useless to hesitate; my symphony must be re-orchestrated. Tied to my bed by fever, I wrote the score in pencil. But my copy was not in time and my symphony will not be given until the next concert.

"Thus my two symphonies will both be performed in the same week. Never before has a professor at the College of Medicine and Surgery found himself in such a position!"

Borodin's second symphony was given for the first time on February 2d, 1877, in the *Rittersaal*, conducted by Naprawnik.

It had no success.

A friendly critic, Monsieur Ivanoff, in the *Novoe Vremya*, said :—

"Listening to this music we recall the memory of the old *bogatyri* (Russian warriors) in all their uncouthness, but also in all their grandeur of character. Even in the tender lyrical passages it is somewhat heavy. These massive forms are at times oppressive and crush the hearer."

It is, in fact, these Russian knights of old, in all their heaviness perhaps, but, above all, in their heroic grandeur, that Borodin has striven to depict.

Monsieur Stassoff tells us this in an article in the *Messager de l'Europe*, published in 1883.*

"Like Glinka," he writes, "Borodin is an epic poet; he is not less national than Glinka, but the Oriental element plays the same part in him as in Glinka, Dargomijsky, Balakireff, Moussorgsky, Rimsky-Korsakoff. He is reckoned among the composers of programme music. Like Glinka, he can say : 'My unfettered imagination needs a text as a positive idea.' Of Borodin's two symphonies, the second is the most perfect, and owes its power not only to the matured talent of its author, but still more to the national character with which its very subject invests it. The old heroic Russian form predominates, as in 'Prince Igor.' I may add that Borodin himself has often told me that in the adagio he intended to recall the songs of the old Slavonic *bayans* (sort of troubadours, or Minnesänger) ; in the first movement, the assembling of the old Russian princes, and in the finale, the banquets of the heroes, to the tones of the *guzla* and bamboo flute, amid the enthusiasm of the people."

The studies to which Borodin had devoted himself for "Prince Igor" were not lost in the working out of his second symphony. At this time his mind was haunted by the picture of feudal Russia,

* "Vingt-cinq Années de l'Art Russe."

and this picture is wonderfully reproduced in the symphony. Much has been said against programme-music. Yet we think that some knowledge of the programme which the author imposed upon his " unfettered imagination," and which has been revealed to us by Monsieur Stassoff, will not detract from the great success which the second symphony has won, first abroad, and afterwards in Russia.

Borodin informed his Belgian friends of this tardy success in a letter dated December 9th, 1885, addressed from St Petersburg to Monsieur and Madame Huberti, who had entertained him in Antwerp at the time of the first performance of the second symphony in Belgium, conducted by Monsieur Huberti :—

" Last week I thought much and kindly of you both. My second symphony was given on Saturday at a symphony-concert. Great heavens ! How it reminded me of the time, still recent, of my visit to you at Antwerp, our first meeting in Brussels, your frank and friendly welcome, which so agreeably surprised and touched me ; it was you that I missed so much, dear friends, you and kind Countess Mercy. Applauded by a most favourable public, I looked round in vain for my Belgian friends. Ah ! how I should have liked to have had you all with me at that moment ! "

But to return to " Prince Igor." We continue to find in Borodin's correspondence traces of the laborious production of this score.

On August 4th, 1879, he again writes to Monsieur Stassoff, from the village of Davidowo in the goverment of Wladimir, where he was spending the holidays :—

" The early part of the summer has not been favourable to the work of composing. I have lost much time in the petty annoyances of life. I have had to live more than a month in the village without Katia, with our two adopted daughters, Lisouchka and Lenotschka. With us, as you know, there is always a fine crop of girls.* We had to live without servants, doing all the work ourselves and dining out. All this has turned me from the service of Apollo, to use the grand style. And yet I have worked. Prince Galitzky, who had only a few phrases of recitative, has now grown into an important character in the opera. I have written for his *rôle* two recitatives and a song of a somewhat cynical character, showing his relations with other people, and especially with Jaroslawna. It is an important addition to the concerted scenes in the first *tableau* of the first act. For the second scene I have written a duet between Galitzky and

* Borodin had several adopted daughters.

Jaroslawna, a chorus of women and a little scene with Jaroslawna. Thus the character of Galitzky has acquired a certain importance.

"I have made him a prince, notwithstanding his brutality, otherwise he would have been a second edition of Skoula. He is a bad man, full of cynicism, but not without a certain dignity.

"I am now working at the finale of the first act. Here I have made a slight change in the original action, which perhaps you will not approve of. I have caused the news of Igor's defeat to be brought, not by merchants, but by the boyards, who may have learned from the merchants of the disaster of the Kayala. They gradually prepare the Princess for the bad news, so that she may not be crushed by it. On hearing it she at first swoons, then, recovering herself, asks from whence the news comes. They tell her it has been brought by travellers who have just arrived, and she has them summoned to her apartments to obtain further details.

"Thus I avoid the recitals of the merchants, and for this reason. If one introduced the entire recital, poetical and picturesque as it may be, it would be long and wearisome, for the public would not understand the words. Moreover, one cannot confide to second-rate singers so fine a piece of musical declamation. Finally, the recital would be poor as compared with the chorus.

"From a scenic point of view, there was perhaps some effect in the reciprocal interruptions of the merchants, but it was very superficial. Besides, it would be difficult to find two singers for these characters, for all the chief performers are engaged. I have already three basses — Kontschak, Skoula and the chamberlain; two baritones—Igor and Galitzky; two tenors — Wladimir and Eroschka. Where am I to find more soloists? Could the places be filled by chorus-singers? Even supposing I could find two soloists, it would be a dead loss. I am an enemy of dualism and dualistic theories in chemistry, in biology, in psychology and in philosophy, as also in the Austro-Hungarian Empire. And yet, as if it were done intentionally, everything with me goes in pairs, like the animals in Noah's Ark. I have two Khans—Kontschak and Gsak; two Wladimirs—Galitzky and Poutivletsky; two women in love — Jaroslawna and Kontschakowna; two fools—Skoula and Eroschka; two brothers—Igor and Wsevolod; two love affairs, two outrages on the princely dignity, two captive princes and two victorious armies of the Polovtsi.

"Besides, would it be possible for the merchants to enter the town without speaking of Igor before they saw the Princess? Is it probable that under

pretence of asking for news, the Princess would
summon the chorus to her apartments ?

" Moreover, the situation of the merchants during
the cries and swooning of the Princess would be
actually ridiculous, and their presence does not
seem to me at all expedient."

Later on he replies to Monsieur Stassoff, who reproached him with the number of choruses in his
opera, by pointing out that the choruses are con-
tantly broken by recitatives and solos, and that they
are necessary to give a rest to the soloist, who is a
human being, not a phonograph, or a barrel-organ
wound up by a key. If she never left the stage and
poured forth unceasingly her highest notes, a singer
would soon be ruined in her prime, unless allowed
some rest.

Let us conclude with the following fragment
from a letter dated from Sokolowo, in the province
of Kostroma, in which Borodin gives a charming
description of the retreat in which he had chosen
to spend the summer of 1880 :—

" I am in the government of Kostroma, in the
district of Kinieschma, eight versts from that town.
I live on a steep and lofty mountain, whose slopes
are washed by the Volga. For thirty versts around
I can see the windings of the river, its verdant
banks, forests, villages, churches and parks, and
then the infinite blue of the immeasurable distance,

it is a marvellous panorama from which one can
hardly withdraw one's gaze.   Unfortunately, I was
not able to get here before the 22d of June.   I
let the time of the lilacs and nightingales go by.

" I came without any heavy baggage, with my
two adopted daughters, Lisouschka and Lenotschka,
whom you probably know.   I have no piano as
yet, and am not quite settled here.   The manor
house which shelters us is a remnant of the old
unreformed Russia, a survival from the ancient
splendour of the feudal lords; it is all falling to
pieces, sinking down and crumbling away.

" The grass grows in the garden ways and shrubs
spread their branches in all directions.   The green
bowers are in ruin, and cheerfulness has fled from
this domain.   On the walls hang, as in dumb reproach, the dingy portraits of the old masters of
the castle, actors and spectators of the joyous scenes
of long ago.   They wear wigs, huge neckties and
enormous rings, and carry gold snuff-boxes, or long
canes with quaint knobs.   They hang on the walls,
moth-eaten, and cast a severe and reproachful look
upon their domain.

" How else should they amuse themselves ?

" Instead of short-haired girls, all sorts of Palasch-
kas and Malaschkas, squatting barefoot, bending
over the stitching of their old-world garments, they
see, in the same rooms, other short-haired girls,

whom they would never have admitted to their table, but who are looked upon as ladies nowadays; these girls are no longer bending over finery, but over treatises upon algebra, and are preparing for their examinations as teachers. Yes; *tempora mutantur*, times are changed, and the apartments that were once the pride of the Russian aristocracy, are now inhabited by lodgers, clerks, or even worse still!

"Unfortunately it is not here alone that the hand of time has fallen so heavily. Neither has it spared the manorial harpsichords. Their wood is worm-eaten, their keys yellowed with age, their wires rusted, their hammers broken. They have made an effort, however, during the last few days, to interpret the musical chaos of our time, but their rust was too ingrained and silence declared their impotence. This annoys me; I must replace them with my summer piano, which has been left with my summer clothes at Davidowo.

"I tell you all this that you may understand how impossible it is for me to occupy myself here with music, and instead of a full-stop at the end of the line, I should like to put a sign of discouragement, if such a thing existed in punctuation."

The extracts from Borodin's correspondence show the obstacles of every kind which retarded the completion of his *magnum opus*. His mind was constantly haunted by this work, and the impossi-

bility of devoting himself to it unremittingly was
not without its effect in darkening the last years
of his life.

"Prince Igor" did not appear until after
Borodin's death. His friends, Rimsky-Korsakoff
and Glazounoff, laboured zealously to complete the
work, and its score was published by Monsieur
Belaïeff at Leipzig in 1889, with a French and
German translation.

Borodin's opera contains beauties of the first order.

Agreeably to the traditions of Russian opera,
which have only been broken by Dargomijsky in
his "Stone Guest," Borodin keeps to the old divisions
into airs, cavatinas, duets and trios.

We must mention, as unrivalled in the strictly
dramatic portion of the work, the cavatina in which
Wladimir invites the fair Kontschakowna to the
love-meeting, the two airs for Jaroslawna and, above
all, the trio in the third act, where Kontschakowna
strives to detain Wladimir by her entreaties, while
Igor recalls his son to a sense of honour and duty.

We must also call attention to that picturesque
portion where Borodin has drawn largely upon the
sources of Oriental music, to which he was no doubt
attracted by hereditary influences. No one has
understood better than he either the charm or the
wildness of these rhythms and harmonies of the
East, against which our senses sometimes rebel, but

which convey to us the profound expression of a civilisation so different from our own. Never has a composer attained a greater vividness of colouring than in the dances of the Polovtsi, where we find, side by side with the rhythmic sonority of the most primitive instruments, the voluptuous charm of the Oriental melodies, combined with the majesty of the songs of victory. We feel that all this belongs to a race and period different to our own; barbarous if you will, but none the less full of grandeur and magnificence, judging by the picture that Borodin has bequeathed to us.

The composer cherished no illusion as to the possibility of ever transplanting this opera to the French stage. We have heard him express himself very decisively on this point at a time when there was a vague proposal for its introduction to Brussels.

"'Prince Igor,'" he then said, "is essentially a national opera which can only interest us Russians who like to renew our patriotism at the very fountain-head of our history, and to see the origins of our nationality revived upon the stage."

Is not this a theme well fitted to inspire the poet and the artist, and might we not more frequently witness the birth of striking works, if all authors, painters, sculptors and composers were animated by such thoughts as these in every country which boasts a distinct nationality?

VIII.

WE have already mentioned the brilliant success which Borodin's first symphony obtained in Germany. This success was poor, however, in comparison with that gained in Belgium by the works of this master in 1885-1886.

At this time the Countess Mercy-Argenteau had undertaken to popularise the works of the New Russian School, and at her initiative three concerts, exclusively devoted to this school, were given during the winter at Liége. These concerts, conducted by Monsieur Th. Jadoul, were very successful, thanks to the judicious selection of the works performed at them, and were the starting point of a movement of popularisation which has had lasting effects.

No works shone more brilliantly than those of Borodin. His first symphony had to be repeated at each concert. Borodin had strongly insisted

that this symphony should be the first of his works
to be performed in Belgium, " so as not to alarm the
public," and this in spite of the entreaties of the
Countess Mercy-Argenteau and others, who would
have preferred to have heard the second symphony,
unquestionably of higher originality.

" I am agreeably surprised," he writes, " that you
should prefer my second symphony to my first.
It is a rare thing; in Europe, as a rule, the preference is given to the first, which is more interesting,
from the technical point of view, as regards musical
science and all those subtleties which pass for the
serious style."

Other works of Borodin were warmly applauded
besides this symphony; we must mention in the
first place his symphonic sketch entitled "In the
Steppes of Central Asia." We have not yet had an
opportunity of speaking of this eminently picturesque work. Composed in 1880, and orginating in
the same inspirations which gave birth to the most
vivid pages in "Prince Igor," it was originally
intended for a representation of *tableaux vivants*
which was to take place in honour of the twenty-
fifth anniversary of the Emperor Alexander II.'s
reign.

It was intended to revive a succession of episodes
in Russian history. Among them all, the picture
illustrated by Borodin's music should have been

specially attractive to the Russian public. Do our
readers wish to know how the critics received this
work which everywhere else compelled the honour
of an encore ?

"In this piece," wrote Monsieur Soloview,* "appears successively a Russian and an Oriental theme,
which at first run separately, but afterwards unite
and move on, linked together, through a scene represented by the music of Félicien David. This work
is not altogether unpleasing, and presents a consoling
contrast to the nonsense of Igor."

Borodin was not in the least prepared for the
success of the Russian concerts at Liége, and his
correspondence with the Countess Mercy-Argenteau
only expresses his diffidence. The following passage from a letter of January 18th, 1885, shows
how he received the news of this triumph, and
expresses his gratitude to the Countess :—

"Russian music is not made to win success. I
am only glad that it has not compromised you.
We Russians, eaters of tallow candles, polar bears,
etc., have too long been consumers of foreign products to be admitted in turn in the character
of producers. Prejudice against Russian products
is very strong and very difficult to uproot, especially
in the domain of art. To do this, it is necessary to

* Professor at the Conservatoire of St Petersburg, and musical
critic.

have taste to appreciate their beauty and originality, courage to overcome prejudice and good sense to know how to do it.   Thanks to a happy coincidence, these three elements are united in you in the highest degree.   In this lies the whole secret of the success of your enterprise."

Together with this letter from Borodin, the Countess Mercy-Argenteau received another written by Liszt and dated from Rome, January 20th, 1885. This letter begins:—

"What a miracle you have just achieved with your Russian concert at Liége, dear, admirable woman !   Materially, the Institute of Deaf and Dumb and Blind has profited; aristically, other deaf and dumb people have heard and spoken, the blind have seen, and looking upon you have been enchanted."

Nothing further was needed to inflame the zeal of this indefatigable lady.

The International Exhibition was about to be opened in Antwerp.   Borodin, impelled on the one hand by his recent success in Liége, and on the other by his scientific tastes, decided to visit the exhibition.   From the time of his arrival in Belgium he found nothing but friends, who knew and appreciated his work and vied with each other for the honour of entertaining and making much of him.   Borodin saw everything through rose-

coloured glasses, and writes to his wife from Liége
in August 1885 :—

" Here I live in clover. Belgium is altogether
like Moscow, and the Belgians Muscovites. Here
amiability and hospitality are overflowing; but this
amiability has nothing conventional about it. It
is ' substantial' as Alexandra Andreïewna would
say. Everyone wants to ask you to dinner, or
offers you a drink, and in these things the Belgians
are true artists. The food and wine are of the first
quality, not as in Germany. The amiability of the
Belgians is especially agreeable, because they have
a charming way of doing you a politeness with
simplicity and heartiness. Germans, French and
English often know how to be amiable beyond
expression, but they are always careful to make
you feel it. They always seem to say : ' I am
amiable to you but you must feel obliged to me in
return.' The Belgian, on the contrary, tries to
avoid every allusion to his superiority, and it
is in this that he is pre-eminently our superior.
Most Belgians are healthy, lively, alert, expansive,
but not without reserve and tact. The Belgian
ladies have, as a rule, a look of health, a pink and
white complexion and fair hair. Among the people,
however, one sees many pretty brunettes with large
eyes and long black lashes. They are a relic of
the Spanish element which has survived to this

day. A sense of dignity and independence is highly developed in every class of society.

"I am literally torn asunder and dragged from breakfasts to dinners and suppers, at which they never fail to give me Russian music, often my own, or that of Cui. It is generally performed respectably, often extremely well, and always conscientiously. I have several times heard my two symphonies and my 'Steppes' played as duets, my songs and my 'Petit poème d'amour d'une jeune fille'*—thus I have christened the seven little pieces intended for the Countess. This little poem is quite the rage."

The organisers of the Antwerp Exhibition had decided to devote a series of concerts to the various schools of modern music. The presence of Borodin was too good an opportunity to be lost, and thanks once again to the influence of Countess Mercy-Argenteau, it was agreed to organise in Antwerp a Russian and a Slavonic concert during his visit to Belgium.

Borodin himself shall relate the history of this time, which was undoubtedly one of the most stirring periods in his existence.

"Do not reproach your gadabout husband," he wrote to his wife on September 21st, 1885, on his

* "Petite Suite," pour deux mains ; pf. solo. Bessel & Co., St Petersburg.

way back to Russia. "The temptation was too
strong for me, miserable sinner; I could not flee
from it. Moreover, it would have been foolish and
prejudicial not only to my own interests, but to
those of Russian music as a whole. It would,
besides, have been uncivil and churlish to refuse
such cordial invitations, such flattering ovations,
as were offered to me in Belgium. I have already
told you that I had been invited officially and
unofficially to conduct the concerts and a festival
given at the Antwerp Exhibition. I was permitted
to fix the programme, the number of rehearsals
and the date, as well as the figure of my fees.
Invitations in the form of letters and telegrams
were sent to me, not only where I *was,* at Liége,
Argenteau and Paris, but even where I *was not,*
as to Spa for example, on the mere report that I
was expected there. I absolutely declined to conduct, on the ground of want of time and the
practice of doing so. Thus I avoided conducting,
but not appearing at the concerts at which my
works were performed. The impossibility of pro-
longing my leave of absence necessitated a change
in the order of the concerts and rehearsals, and the
Exhibition Committee were even on the point of
officially addressing the Russian government with
a view to getting my furlough extended.

"Many people interested in my compositions came

to hear them and make my personal acquaintance.
Thus Madame Lynen, wife of the President of the
Exhibition, an old pupil of Liszt and a great
admirer of my works, came back from Baden-Baden
on purpose. A great number of amateurs, composers and professors, etc., came to Antwerp from
Liége, Brussels, Ghent, Spa, Holland and France.

"In consequence of my refusal, two conductors
offered spontaneously to conduct my symphonies.
Professor G. Huberti of Brussels chose No. 2, the
director of the Liége Conservatoire, Monsieur
Radoux, chose the first for the Festival of September 19th.* I will mention one very characteristic fact. Just imagine! The German colony
did all in their power to prevent the performance
of my second symphony; is it not singular, and
just what happens in our country? But every
obstacle was overcome. On September 9th, 'The
Steppes' was performed, on the 16th the second
symphony, and the symphony No. 1 on the 19th;
besides these, 'The Sea,' 'The Sleeping Beauty'
and 'The Sea Queen.' The ovations went *crescendo* from concert to concert. They were as
unanimous on the part of the public as on that
of the orchestral leaders and the committee. I

* In one of his letters, Borodin attributes to Monsieur Radoux
a phrase which is very characteristic of his work. "There is a man
who does not strive to make Russian music; it exudes from every
pore."

was obliged to make a speech and address the orchestra :—

"'It is now my turn, gentlemen, to thank you heartily for so flattering a welcome, and for the honour you have done me; believe me, gentlemen, there is no greater reward for a composer than to hear his work performed by such an orchestra as yours!'

"The words produced a fresh outburst of enthusiasm. I have now learned to speak and to write in French words that really come from the heart.

"On September 20th, that is yesterday, declining all invitations, visits, etc., I fled to Antwerp.

"My dear godmother,* who came specially to the two last concerts in Antwerp, was radiant at the triumph of Russian music which she had introduced into Belgium. She is a woman highly endowed, charming in every way, and very remarkable for the versatility of her talents. If she were not getting on for fifty, one would be sure to fall in love with her."

During his visit to Belgium, Borodin made many friends, and was obliged to promise to return and preside once more over the performance of his works in Brussels and Liége. An opportunity soon presented itself. The Countess Mercy-Argenteau

* Countess Mercy-Argenteau.

had succeeded in persuading the directors of the theatre at Liége to accept an opera by Cui—" The Prisoner of the Caucasus." The first performance had been fixed for the Christmas holidays, in order that Monsieur Cui might take part in the final rehearsals and the performance of his work. On the other hand, a new Russian concert was to be given by the Société d'Emulation of Liége, and Borodin's second symphony was to be performed at a popular concert in Brussels and at the Conservatoire of Liége. This was quite enough to induce Borodin to accompany his colleague to Belgium.

Madame Borodin, whose health obliged her to escape from the climate of St Petersburg, was wintering at Moscow. On December, 7th 1885, Borodin informs her of his decision :—

"To-day I will answer your questions—shall I return to you for the Christmas holidays, and why is Pawlitch* leaving? Do not be angry with me, dear dove, I shall not be able to come to you, and shall not be with you before the Carnival and Easter. It is in this way : during the holidays the first performance of 'The Prisoner of the Caucasus' will take place at Liége; then a concert by the Société d'Emulation, at which will be given frag-

---

* Monsieur Dianine, a favourite pupil, and Borodin's successor at the Academy of Medicine.

ments of 'Igor,' of the 'Pskovitaine,' of 'Angelo,'
my 'Steppes,' and songs by Cui and myself.

"At the Conservatoire, my symphony in B minor
will be performed under most favourable auspices,
with Radoux as conductor. This symphony will
also be given at Brussels, under the direction of
Dupont, by an unusually fine orchestra. The Count
and Countess d'Argenteau, and all my friends in
Liége, Brussels and Antwerp, insist upon my going
with Cui. The latter, like all our friends in St
Petersburg, musicians or otherwise, as well as all
our relatives, urge me with the same insistence.
The publishers defray the expenses of the journey
both ways. The Count and Countess offer their
hospitality at Argenteau.

"I did not write to you about it sooner, because
I was undecided, and wavered for a long time.
Now I have made up my mind, but on one condition, which is that Pawlitch shall spend the
holidays with you, especially as he will not have
time to go later on.

"I know too well from the Antwerp Exhibition
how important is the presence of the composer on
such occasions. So we are starting, Cui and I, and
shall return together. Such a journey is not forgotten in a lifetime. I know that from my Antwerp
experience. Forgive me then, dear dove. I am now
fifty-one, and God knows if such an opportunity

may occur again. Do not show this letter to anyone, dear; they would think I was boasting."

Arrived in Belgium, Borodin and Cui had no
longer a moment to themselves, and Borodin's correspondence betrays a condition of bewilderment
produced by rehearsals, concerts, invitations, visits
and ovations of all sorts.

Arriving at Liége on December 25th, 1885
(Russian style), Borodin, at the close of the first
day, writes to his wife :—

"I send you my greetings, dear dove, and my best
wishes for your birthday. To think we are separated by a distance of more than 3100 versts! It
is terrible to say so, but these 3100 versts have not
seemed long to me, and we are not tired, thanks to
the comfort of first-class travelling and sleeping
cars, to which I am not accustomed. At Berlin we
had a few hours' break and we wandered about,
which rested us a great deal.

"At half-past twelve in the day, after having
lunched, we went on by the express. A great
feeling of sadness came over me. Fancy, the rivers
are free from ice and the grass is green. Beyond
Berlin a little snow, but such strange snow, not in
the least wintry; the sky and air are spring like,
as with us in April. The fields are green and one
walks out in an autumn overcoat. Only, towards
evening it grows more chilly and my pelisse has

not been too much to keep off the draughts in the railway carriage.

"At 10.40 we reached Cologne, and at 2.24 a.m. we arrived at Liége, twenty minutes late. Thanks to the kind offices of Monsieur Albert Gœthals, the translator of 'The Prisoner of the Caucasus,' we found two rooms at the hotel, opening one into the other, well warmed and with excellent beds.

"Letters from de Gœthals and the Countess awaited us. The Countess, all joy, agitation and emotion wrote that she would be with us at eleven o'clock, and invited us to breakfast before the rehearsal of the opera.

"Punctually at eleven she appeared, radiant, sprightly, really handsome. We chatted a little and went to breakfast at the Café Vénitien near the hotel; then to the rehearsal of 'The Prisoner of the Caucasus.'

"Cui seated himself at the piano and accompanied, singing with the performers.

"At night we were at the rehearsal for the concert of the Société d'Emulation. The Countess, like a true brood hen, never left us, one on her right and one on her left. After the rehearsal, Cui had to stay at the hotel to go through the parts with the artists of the theatre. But the Countess carried me off to the Château d'Argenteau, where I found myself in the same room as last autumn.

" During the day I met a number of acquaintances in Liége, who received me with open arms. I received so many invitations, that if I went to all these dinners and suppers I should not get back to Russia before February.

" The newspapers speak of our arrival in Belgium, the music shops display our works, and those of Korsakoff and Glazounoff. Among others I saw my septet published. I will bring it back to you.

" The honour paid us is inconceivable.

"All the seats are taken,and are even at a premium. A French critic has published a detailed analysis of my second symphony, with quotations from the score. It is more eulogistic than any which has yet been written. Dupont, director of the theatre and popular concerts at Brussels, has made an appointment in order to go over the second symphony with me, which obliges me to spend to-morrow night in Brussels."

In a subsequent letter, Borodin gives an account of the Russian concert given by the Société d'Emulation.

" Yesterday, Friday, Cui entertained the Count and Countess at dinner at the hotel. He is not a poor beggar as I am.

" At eight o'clock in the evening the Russian concert of the Société d'Emulation took place. They performed ' Antar,' fragments of ' Angelo,' of 'La Pskovitaine,' the 'Steppes,' the cavatina of Wladimir Igorewitch, and the finale of the 'Prisoner of the Caucasus.'

"Cui and I were recalled enthusiastically after the performance of our works; mine had to be repeated in deference to the public demand. After the concert, the Count and Countess, with Cui and myself, spent the evening with Monsieur Habets, President of the Musical Committee of the Société d'Emulation. The cream of musical society in Liége were gathered there, and we were literally overwhelmed with compliments. We had some music, and our works were charmingly performed. One lady in particular sang my cavatina remarkably well, with all the sentiment and spirit which it admits of."

The next day he again reverts to the success of the previous night.

"After the concert, the compliments and ovations were continued in various forms. I was besieged with demands for autographs. One young lady pursued me even into the street as we left the concert room. I could not, however, satisfy her. The next day she applied to the Countess by letter, enclosing an addressed envelope and a stamp.

"After this, my headquarters were no longer Liége, but Brussels, where my second symphony was being performed. It was first given on

Saturday in the Salle de la Grande Harmonie (chiefly on account of the English, because they will not listen to profane music on Sunday), then on Sunday at the Theatre de la Monnaie, for the Belgians.   The ovations paid me surpass, according to what I am told in Brussels, anything which has happened before at the performance of a symphony.

"Cui's suite was also much applauded (it is very different from Moscow).   We had to bow from our box, and as we left the theatre a party of young people cried : ' *Vivent les Russes! vive la Russie!* '

.   .   .   .

"Then the basis of operations was again removed to Liége.   To-day the first performance of ' The Prisoner of the Caucasus ' took place.   It is suitably put on the stage, but the choruses were weak and the dances were enough to make your hair stand on end.

"My success in Brussels has a special significance, because the Conservatoire and the musicians are on our side.   Dupont has pressed me to send him everything that I do, and particularly the score and translation of ' Prince Igor,' which he wants to produce in Brussels.   The publishers themselves are not ashamed to offer us their services."

On the 2d of January (Russian style), after the first performance of the " Prisoner of the Caucasus," he writes :—

" The opera has had a great success and Cui was twice recalled with enthusiasm.

" On his last appearance the artists presented him with a gilded lyre. The opera went fairly well. · The baritone, bass, soprano and tenor were excellent, and, what is still better, their voices blended, so that the concerted pieces were perfect. The choruses were pitiable. As to the dances, the deuce knows what they were like ; one dancer was even hissed. The costumes were laughable. The Tcherkesse costume with the cartridge bags and fur cap was all right, but the rest were the very devil ! The women were neither dressed like Russians, Tartars, nor Georgians. The prisoner himself was dressed like a coachman without sleeves. It was very amusing. The orchestra is fairly good and the leader of it seems a worthy man.

" A host of celebrities, musical, theatrical and literary, attended the first performance.

" This opera will probably be given in Brussels, but ' Angelo ' is also being negotiated for. To give you an idea of the interest taken in Russian compositions, I must tell you that several people came from Paris yesterday to see the ' Prisoner of the Caucasus.' One lady had studied the whole opera from the pianoforte score and knew it by heart, as well as my two symphonies."

Such is the history of this professional tour, which left enduring traces behind it in the diffusion of Russian music beyond the frontiers of that empire.   The enthusiasm which then reached its climax has, of necessity, abated.   The Countess Mercy d'Argenteau is unfortunately no longer with us to uphold and animate it with the zeal of a neophyte.   But Russian music has taken root in our symphony concerts, at which, in Brussels as at Liége, some new work from St Petersburg is annually given.   It may even be said that the works of Borodin have become classics in Belgium, and will keep their place in the repertory of its orchestral and chamber concerts.

At a banquet after the Popular Concert in Brussels, which Monsieur Rimsky-Korsakoff was invited to conduct in 1890, Monsieur Radoux, director of the Conservatoire at Liége, claimed for the latter town, and more especially for the Countess Mercy d'Argenteau, the honour of having started in Belgium a movement which contributed in a great measure to the success of the new Russian School in Europe.   The Countess was not indifferent to this toast, and wrote to him from St Petersburg the following lines :—

" DEAR MASTER,—Although I have only just returned to Argenteau, I will not put off for a day the pleasure of thanking you for your friendly remembrance. I was near you in my thoughts during Korsakoff's tour. I had no doubt as to the warm welcome he would receive, nor of the success of the superb concerts among musicians and cultivated people; but I did not dream that my memory would be so delicately and so affectionately recalled at this fine musical feast. Thanks with all my heart. I was touched beyond all expression."

The success which Borodin achieved abroad, and particularly in Belgium, was certainly the greatest artistic enjoyment which he was permitted to experience.

Of this we need no other proof than the following letter, written a few months before his death, May 6th, 1886, to his old friend Gavrouschkiewitch, at whose house we saw him begin his artistic career. This letter shows how much he was impressed by these later successes, and affords a pleasant contrast to the tone of discouragement pervading the correspondence which we have quoted in the preceding chapters :—

"I thank you from my heart for the kind remembrance which you have kept of your humble servant, who is most guilty in replying so tardily.

"You have not changed, and I am pleased to find that you have kept your freshness, your humour, your passion for music, and, above all, sufficient vigour to play the 'cello, which is by no means easy.   As to myself, I abandoned that instrument long since; first, because I always played it very badly; truth is truth, and it was only from an amiable condescension that you tolerated me at your parties; secondly, because I have had other occupations in my artistic career in which I am generally considered more apt as a composer than as a virtuoso.   I have been fairly successful in this capacity, especially abroad.

"There, my two symphonies obtained a success which I was far from expecting.   The first E in flat major was given with great success at festivals and concerts in Baden-Baden, Leipzig, Dresden, Rostock, Antwerp, Liége, etc.; it won for me a solid reputation abroad.   The second in B minor pleased, especially in Belgium.   At the Popular Concerts in Brussels it was repeated by desire and performed at two successive concerts, a most unusual event, which had never occurred since the inauguration of those concerts.

"It had an equally great success at Liége, and at the Antwerp Exhibition.   This year it will be performed at Sondershausen, at the festival of the Allgemeiner Musikverein.   This symphony has certainly increased my reputation as a composer.

"But the most popular of my works abroad is my

symphonic sketch—'Dans les Steppes de l'Asie Centrale.' It has gone the round of Europe from Christiania to Monaco, and in spite of its patriotic programme (the success of Russian arms in Asia), this work has been encored almost everywhere and often repeated by desire, as at the Strauss concerts in Vienna and the Lamoureux concerts in Paris.

"My first quartet pleased not only in Europe (at Carlsruhe, Leipzig, Liége, Brussels, Antwerp, etc.), but also in America. During the present season it was performed four times by the Philharmonic Society of Buffalo, an unusual success for a foreign composition.

"I learn also that my vocal compositions are generally successful; but beware of the evil eye! Personally I play all instruments, but all as badly as in old days. I am still very fond of quartets and chamber-music, but now I am content to listen.

"To-day, however, I scraped the 'cello, and though I had not touched my instrument for eleven years, I played, with my wife and a friend from Moscow, Mendelssohn's trio in D minor and Reissiger's E minor trio. I certainly played very badly, but with perseverance and the sweat of my brow.

"I always remember with pleasure, dear Ivan Ivanitch, you and your evenings, which I so enjoyed, and which were such a serious school for me. I recall them with gratitude. I remember, too, the excellent pastry which we washed down with 'Evêque,' as it amused you to call the 'Bisschof.' I heartily wish you success in everything, health, long life, and every enjoyment.—I remain always your friend, and heartily sign myself, YOUR BAD SECOND 'CELLO."

I X.

DEATH OF BORODIN.   POSTHUMOUS WORKS.

THESE tardy successes stirred in Borodin the genius of composition.   From this period date the scherzo in B flat, for orchestra, dedicated to Monsieur Th. Jadoul, the andante in the form of a Spanish serenade, a string quartet on the notes B-la-f, dedicated to his friend (Monsieur Belaïeff) on his birthday, for which Rimsky-Korsakoff wrote the first allegro, Liadoff the scherzo, and Glazounoff the finale, and lastly a second string quartet.

The autumn of 1886 was, however, particularly depressing to him.   He spent the greater part of it at Moscow attending upon his wife, who was seriously ill in a suburb of the town, and his mother-in-law, for whom Borodin had a filial affection and who was ill in the town itself. Shortly afterwards she died, and it is easily understood that until the end of the winter of 1886 Borodin was occupied with other things than music.

He had scarcely recovered, and was busying himself with the composition of a third symphony, when death cut short a career which leaves behind it indelible traces alike in the art and science of Russia.   On February 14th, 1887, he wrote to his wife, still detained by illness in Moscow :—

"To-morrow we have a musical party here, it will be very grand—'*il y aura de la bougie,*' as Murger would say in his 'Vie de Bohéme'; to-day we have engaged the pianist.   There will be a masked ball, but I will not unveil the mysteries, and I leave the description of the entertainment to the more skilful pens of your other correspondents."

The party took place.   Borodin was dressed in the national costume, with red shirt and high boots; he was talking, full of animation, with his guests, when he was seen to stagger forward. Without a cry, and without suffering, he succumbed in a few seconds to a ruptured aneurism, in the presence of his guests, who were thrown into consternation.

He now reposes on the banks of the Neva, in the Nevsky Monastery, the Westminster Abbey of Russia, side by side with his friend Modeste Moussorgsky, who had preceded him to the grave by several years.

His friends have raised him a worthy monument.   At the back of his bust in bronze, in the

style of a cenotaph, Borodin's chief themes are
reproduced in mosaic on a gold background—
The first theme of the first symphony, the chorus
of the Polovtsian women from the first act of
" Prince Igor," the first bars from the " Chanson de la
Forêt Sombre," the first theme from the scherzo of
the third symphony (unfinished), and the first bars
from " Les Steppes," as well as an enlarged facsimile
of his signature. The monument which bears this
golden page from the musical history of Russia is
surmounted by a Georgian cross and constructed
of Serdobol granite. At the foot of the pedestal
lie the *guzla* and the *goudok*, the two national
instruments which play so important a part in the
second symphony and in " Prince Igor."

The wrought-iron grating which encloses the
mausoleum bears the monogram A. B. upon a scroll
between three crowns. The first is inscribed with
chemical formulas; the second with themes from
his musical works, and the third is formed of a
branch of laurel which encircles the double crown
(artistic and scientific) of Borodin.

A few weeks after this fatal termination of a life
which had known only the highest aspirations in
art and science, Monsieur Rimsky-Korsakoff con-
voked, in Borodin's own house, the friends of this
illustrious artist, whose portrait, placed on a table
beside a pile of manuscript music, seemed to preside

over this mournful gathering. Rimsky-Korsakoff proposed to undertake the revision and publication of the unfinished works. Among these the most important was "Prince Igor." There were also fragments of the third symphony, upon which Borodin was hard at work at the time of his death, the second string quartet, a few songs, etc.

Rimsky-Korsakoff was well fitted to carry out this great undertaking. He had been for many years the intimate friend of Borodin, who liked to consult him upon his works, and who had allowed him to hear them from their embryo stage to the moment of their full completion. No one was better fitted than himself to assist in their revision, as he had already done for the "Stone Guest" of Dargomijsky and the "Khovanschtchina" of Moussorgsky. This pious task was unanimously accorded to him. He was efficiently assisted by Monsieur Glazounoff, who accomplished the feat of re-writing from memory the overture to "Prince Igor," besides the two movements of the third symphony, of which only a few fragments of manuscript were in existence.

All the songs left in manuscript by Borodin have been prepared for publication and engraved. These posthumous songs are mostly far inferior to the first series of eight, and with the exception of one, entitled "An Arab Melody," which is full of colour and expression, and in which he makes use of his study of the texts of Arab songs in the Public Library at St Petersburg, it is doubtful if Borodin would have published them during his lifetime.

It is not so with the fragments of the third symphony and the second string quartet, which contain beauties of the highest order.

X.

THE MAN.

MADAME CATHARINE SERGEIEWNA BORODIN only survived her husband by a few months. She died July 28th, 1887.

It was after this event that Monsieur Stassoff was put in possession of the long correspondence addressed by Borodin to his wife. We will only extract one more letter, of an intimate nature and relating neither to art nor science, but which, in the opinion of his friends, depicts more truly than any other page of his correspondence the heart and soul of the poet, the character and moral physiognomy of the man.

Here is the letter, which needs no commentary.

"HEIDELBERG, *July* 30*th*, 1877.

" I have never been so far from you and yet I have never been so close. You will understand, I am at Heidelberg !

.   .   .   .

"I spent a day and a half at Bonn; I will not describe them to you, for they would not be of interest. From thence I started by the Rhenish line for the Promised Land, Mecca, Medina, Jerusalem, call it what you will—Heidelberg!!

"I have seen once more that panorama of the Rhine, those well-known banks which we visited together, from Bonn to Mayence. I have seen our Bingen again. Do you remember it? Heavens! How I have lived again through all our impressions of that time!

"After Mayence I revisited Bensheim, Heppenheim, etc., where we went so often.

"I was so moved that I never noticed the time. Only long afterwards I remembered that I had neither eaten nor drunk since six o'clock in the morning, in spite of the heat which was overwhelming. I devoured with my eyes every hill, every footpath, every cottage and village; all recalled those happy days. As I approached Heidelberg I was obliged to look out of the carriage window to hide my gathering tears and make an effort not to sob like a child. With a swelling heart I looked out for the little garden running down to the railroad, where I saw you the day after Wolfsbrunnen. Do you remember it? At last I found it! I recognised it at once; I knew its perfume! No doubt it has happened to you to

dream of places which you seem to have known for
ages past, where you know beforehand what you
are going to see, where you hasten to examine
every corner, convinced that nothing of it is new to
you. Such was my dream at this moment.

"I jumped into the omnibus and drove straight
to the Badischer Hof, where I stopped for the first
time in 1859, and I dined at the *table d'hôte*.
Here is the Hauptstrasse; next I shall see the
Darmstädter Hof, then Derara, then the Goldner
Engel; everything, to the smallest detail, is revived
in my memory. Now we are at the Karpfengasse,
the dear Karpfengasse where you came to see me
for the first time. Do you recall it? There I
showed you my linen cupboard; I could think of
nothing more witty to say to you at the moment.
There Erlenmeyer's laboratory used to be. Here
at last is the Badischer Hof, the old room, the old
staircase. I engaged a room, and when left to myself I could not help crying like a child. I cannot
say what a flood of different emotions suddenly
came upon me.

"After having dressed, I remembered that it was
dinner-time and went down to the dining-room.

"Unconsciously, mechanically, I sat down in the
same place which I had occupied at the table seventeen years ago. After dining in haste I rose pre-
cipitately to visit the 'Holy Places'; first of all

the Castle. What did I not feel as I went over the same walks and pathways where we wandered together in those first days of our happiness? What would I not have given to have you with me just then? There it was! the sombre, melancholy, shadowy pathway with stone arches through which we glided one evening. Do you remember how you clung closer to me, half afraid?

" I should have liked to have gone to Hoffmann's, to the little house with the old worm-eaten stair-case. I should have liked to, but I did not dare to ask for it. What if the little house had ceased to exist? What if the name of Hoffmann was forgotten? Here is St Peter's Church, where you heard ' St Paul ' when I took part in the orchestra. Here is the Museum, where you often went to the rehearsals. Here is the confectioner's, where we met the Koudascheffs, the little house in which the Sorokines used to live, No. 12 in the Fried-richstrasse, where I lived before our marriage, the room where I lived with Mendeleïeff; here is the house where Anna Paulovna Bruner lived and died, and where I made the acquaintance of Sophie Karlowna; and No. 6 in the Karpfenstrasse, Erlenmeyer's laboratory. Here I could restrain myself no longer. I went into the courtyard. The laboratory no longer exists, but the buildings are intact. I saw the place where I used to work.

" Here is No. 2, my little lodging, where the linen cupboard was. . . . I wanted to go in, but I saw an old woman knitting German fashion, one finger in the air ; I was alarmed and fled.

" I wandered aimlessly till nightfall, examining every nook and corner. I could not believe that it was all real, that I was really among these familiar haunts. I touched the walls, the locks, the steps. I behaved like a man half-witted.

" The next day I went first to visit the specialists, then I went back to my place at the *table d'hôte.*

" It seemed to me that I ate the same dishes as seventeen years ago. I found them quite to my taste. The chair on which I sat seemed extremely comfortable ; it was a cane chair, to which I felt quite accustomed. In a word, it was *my* chair, and my neighbours at table seemed old friends though I saw them for the first time.

" After dinner I started straight by the heavenly path to Mecca, that is to say to Wolfsbrunnen· The road was as familiar to me as the fingers on my own hands, but it seemed to me it had been swept and widened for my coming. At the Wolfs-brunnen I found everything in the old order. They have simply added a covered gallery. I sat down opposite the basin in which the trout were swimming. The water still flows in four streams from the wolves' jaws, just as it has flowed uninterruptedly for seventeen years. A great deal of water must have flowed away since then.

"A young girl of fifteen came towards me, smiling. Doubtless she was going to say,—

"'At last you have come back! Why have you been absent so long?' Not so, however.

"'Will you take beer, or anything else?' was her inquiry.

"She did not recognise me! How could she, seeing she was not born in those days.

"I dare not attempt to describe all I felt as I sat before the fountain, gazing fixedly at the water which fell ceaselessly with a monotonous rhythm into the basin where the silly fish swim apathetically, awaiting the frying-pan. What were my thoughts! What mingled joy and bitterness. . . . I sat a long while over my *schoppen* of beer, then I arose and took, without hesitation, the road at the bottom of the valley that skirts the Neckar, that same road by which we returned to Heidelberg together. In vain I looked for the stones on which we sat, and the rock near the gate of the town where I seized you like a lunatic and knocked down your umbrella. The ruthless hand of progress has destroyed these relics and planted a railway line all along the river. The sight of this depressed me. Only the gateway, the Karlsthor, is left standing. I passed and repassed under its arch several times, to the great astonishment of the passers-by. Weary, weighed down by a crowd of memories, I returned heavy-footed to my room and threw myself on my bed, where I soon slept like the dead.

"The sun was high above the horizon when I awoke. I went about my business; then, in company with Monsieur Lossen, professor of chemistry, I went as far as the Molkenkur and returned by the Schloss. But what was Lossen doing there? He understood nothing whatever about it.

"It was not till afternoon that I recovered my senses, and after having looked up Hoffmann's address in a directory, I made my way rapidly towards the Holy of Holies. What have the Germans done? The old Bergheimerstrasse no longer exists even in their memories; it has become a sort of Liteïnaïa, of Twerskaïa,* of Hauptstrasse—houses upon houses, and still houses! I sought in vain for No. 14; it exists no longer. At last, in a little street running across it, I found the holy dwelling. I drew near with a beating heart.

"'Does Monsieur le Professeur Hoffmann live here?'

"'The Professor died a fortnight ago.'

* Two main streets, the former in St Petersburg, the latter in Moscow.

"It was short and to the point. The answer almost overwhelmed me.

"'Frau Professorin is at home, shall I announce you?'

"Sophie Petrowna appeared in mourning, and received me in a friendly way; she was glad to see me. In a few words she gave me the details of her husband's death, who had succumbed after an attack of apoplexy. She told me that she had a pension, and spoke of her children. Little Mary is married in London; she is already the mother of another little Mary. Heinrich (you remember the one Bogdan Marko-Wowtchok flung into the rain-water tank one day?) has been living in Hamburg for some time past. Charley, little Charley, whose life I saved by extracting a piece of glass from his throat, is finishing his studies at the Ecole Poly-technique.

"I went into the dining-room; intact this dear old room with its dear old long table; intact, too—like preserves—the thin misses and madams board-ing in the house, talking like Lichatcheff as they decorously and ceremoniously sipped their coffee.

"Sophie Petrowna asked after you with interest, and introduced me to her little English niece, Loulou (*sic*). Loulou, though young and pretty, is a hybrid creature. She was born and grew up in Moscow, was educated in Heidelberg, and lives in

London. In short, the devil alone knows of what
nationality she may be. I was told she was engaged to a Russian doctor named Bedriaga.

"Dr Bedriaga himself was not long in putting in
an appearance. He is a young adolescent, doctor
of philosophy in the University of Jena. A
Muscovite, a passionate music-lover and a good
pianist; the nephew, fancy, of Rimsky-Korsakoff.

"This was a whole series of common interests
between us. He knew me by name. He is a
charming fellow. He is studying zoology, but
spends his time at the Wolfsbrunnen and Speyerhof,
madly in love with his *fiancée*. Naturally I could
not help comparing their romance with ours. I
put myself completely in his place, which at once
drew us together like old friends.

"We went into the garden together, *our* garden,
where we met the day after Wolfsbrunnen. Alas!
the little seat has long ceased to exist, but on the
whole the garden remains what it used to be, only
the flowers of poetry and love have given place to
cabbages and cucumbers, abundantly planted by
the providential hand of the housekeeper, Sophie
Petrowna.

"She invited me to tea, but I declined in order to
go to the Speyerhof in the evening. She then
asked me to dinner the next day. I accepted, and
having said good-bye to Madame, I made a

pilgrimage to the cemetery, as I did once before with you. Alas! here again the utilitarian Germans have so civilised the place as to make it barely recognisable, as. is nearly everywhere the case in the suburbs of Heidelberg. In all directions the roads have become magnificent; one can drive everywhere, even to the Königstuhl. The donkeys of old Heidelberg are forgotten.

"Must I tell you the impressions I felt at the Speyerhof? They were necessarily the same as at the Wolfsbrunnen, though less intense.

"The next day Sophie Petrowna set before me a fish pie in the Muscovite fashion, and gave me a quantity of news of old acquaintances in Heidelberg.

"This, my beloved, is an account of where and how I find myself. I kiss you 00 times, which signifies an infinite number of times, multiplied an infinite number of times by itself. Try to work out the sum. But I must make haste and finish. Embrace the mother. Now to Wurzburg and Munich, thence to Jena and home! I shall only stop at Wilna.   Ton Moi."

Liège.

Mon cher Monsieur,

Je ne pouvais pas vous remercier plus tôt de votre aimable envoi — je vous serre la main en commençant, puisque je vous prie d'agréer l'expression de toute ma sympathie. De Bruxelles (les dernières) maintenant que je m'envole de vous souvenir, vous savez déjà combien vous m'avez écrit pour mon quatuor et pour ma symphonie — et bien merci, grâce à cette exécution les plus grands maîtres et qu'elle produit un effet, aussi quelle grand effet qu'il ne m'a fallu

Bien. Je vous remercie encore. Davantage pour l'intérêt personnel que vous avez pour l'œuvre même et pour l'opinion flatteuse que vous avez pour ma musique en général.

L'appréciation de ma musique par un musicien de valeur comme vous est d'une grande importance pour moi et je ne saurais trop vous en remercier. Veuillez bien cher maître et me pense's-y gardez-vous fidèle à votre très dévoué A. de Borodine.

PREFACE TO SECOND PART.

In 1877 Borodin visited Germany with two of his pupils, a sort of scientific and artistic pilgrimage, taking the German universities by the way, with Weimar as the final goal.

At this time Liszt was the reigning monarch there; it is his court and his school that Borodin describes in private letters addressed to his wife. These letters are highly interesting, not only because they show us Liszt in a new and unknown light, but also because they help us to understand more thoroughly the judgment of the master upon Borodin's works.

We know that Liszt had a high opinion of the new Russian school, and especially of Borodin. This opinion is frequently expressed in these private letters which were never written for publication and cannot therefore impeach the extreme modesty of their author.

Borodin had occasion to see Liszt again in 1881 at the Magdeburg Festival, of which he wrote an account to Monsieur C. Cui, in which he was unfortunately interrupted. After this festival he again visited Weimar; a letter to Madame Borodin describes his last interview with Liszt and completes the incomparable portrait which he has given us of the great Hungarian master.

We give a literal translation of the chief passages in these letters.

II.

FRANZ LISZT.

As Sketched in the Letters of Borodin.

To face page 106.

I.

LETTER TO MADAME BORODIN.

JENA, *July* 3d, 1877.

. . . At the furthest end of the town we have found, for ten thalers a month, a lodging with service, beds and bedding. We shall soon have a piano. The view is divine : all around us are gardens ; behind the house are fields and meadows. The air is excellent. To-night we expect Goldstein, who is coming from Leipzig, and we shall make tea for the first time.

Imagine that for half a day Alexandrouschka has seen just in front of him, . . . guess who ? But it all deserves a detailed description, so I will begin *ab ovo*.

On the 30th of June we stayed at the hotel and read the papers, when suddenly I saw that there would be a concert of church music in the Cathedral of Jena on July 2d, with several novelties in the programme, among others four numbers by

Liszt :—" Benedictus " for piano, organ and violin ;
" Ave maris stella " for male chorus, with organ ;
" Ave Maria " for organ, " Cantico del Sole " for
baritone and chorus, with organ and piano; and
into the bargain (how did it come to figure in a
programme of church music ?) Chopin's " Funeral
March," arranged by Liszt for piano, organ and
violoncello !

Obviously, we could not do otherwise than hasten
to the ticket-office, where we learnt that Liszt, who
was at Weimar, would come to Jena to take part
in the concert.

I at once resolved to pay him a visit the very
next day, which I had been meditating for several
days past, but invariably postponed.

From Jena to Weimar is only about three
quarters of an hour by train; much the same
distance as from St Petersburg to Tarkoë-Selo.

On Sunday, July 1st, that is to say on the following day, I started at 11.51.

Calculating that Liszt would dine about one
o'clock, like everybody else in Germany, I decided
to dine on my arrival and to call on him afterwards.
No one could give me his address. Finally I learnt in
a *bric-à-brac* shop—Marienstrasse 1/17, quite at the
end of the town near the park.

I went there, but mistaking the door, I rang
opposite and inquired for Liszt's apartment.

" What Liszt ?   No Liszt lives here."

" Not hereabouts ? "

" No, we know everybody who lives in this quarter. Colonel Weinert lives here, next door Lieutenant Winkler or Winkel, etc.   Anna! Anna ! " cried the German whom I was questioning, " the gentleman is asking if anyone of the name of Liszt lives in this neighbourhood."

A lanky, uncouth person joined in the conversation.

" Wait a bit ! It strikes me that a certain Dr Liszt lives across the way."

I went opposite to a little corner house, two-storied, covered with a green vine, behind an iron fence.   The gate opened into a neat little garden, where a gentleman was walking, in a straw hat.

" Does Dr Liszt live here ? "

" Yes, he lives here, but he is at table.   After dinner he rests and does not receive till half-past four."

" Bad luck ! " I whispered to myself, and I went wandering through the town.

Every street, every square recalls the art of the past. Glorious past ! There is the house where old Goethe died in 1832, after dwelling there for fifty-six years.   Here is a house simple in appearance, but old-fashioned in style ; above the door one reads the simple inscription—" Here Schiller

dwelt." He died there in 1805. There is the room
in which he worked, furnished as in his lifetime.
Not far from there is the cemetery, where, in the
same chapel, beside the grand dukes, the ashes of
the two great poets repose beneath two oaken
monuments decorated with laurel wreaths.

Here is Wieland's house, and further on that of
Herder. What thinkers, poets, creative geniuses
have dwelt in this microscopic town!

Having wandered about until half-past four I
return to the Marienstrasse, to the iron wicket I
had had so much trouble to find. I opened the gate
and prepared my visiting card. The man in the
straw hat was no longer in the garden, but his
place was occupied by two ladies, one of whom,
judging by her dress, did not look like a German.

"Can I see the Herr Doctor?" I inquired, airing
my German.

"Oh, yes! On the first floor."

Heaven be praised! I rushed to the stairs, when
I found I had lost my card. I had not another.
I went back to look for it and even went through
the gate. One of the ladies ran after me, holding
out the card which I had dropped.

"Is this the card you are looking for?"

I thanked her, lifting my hat respectfully, very
high in the air, quite in German fashion, and went
once more upstairs. I felt as though I were going

to consult a doctor in his own house. Scarcely had I sent in my card when there arose before me, as though out of the ground, a tall figure with a long nose, a long black frock-coat and long white hair.

"You have written a fine symphony," growled the tall figure, in a resonant voice and in excellent French; and he stretched out a long hand and a long arm. "Welcome, I am delighted to see you. Only two days ago I played your symphony to the Grand Duke, who was charmed with it. The first movement is perfect. Your *andante* is a *chef-d'œuvre*. The scherzo is enchanting. . . and then this passage is so ingenious."

And then his long fingers began to peck (*picorer*), to use a picturesque expression which Moussorgsky made use of to describe the progression of distant intervals, pizzicato, in the scherzo and finale of my first symphony. He ran on incessantly; his strong hand caught my own and held me down to a sofa where there was nothing left for me to do but nod approval and lose myself in thanks.

The fine face of the old man, with its energetic, vivacious features, was uplifted before me, while he talked incessantly, overwhelming me with questions, passing from French to German and *vice versâ*.

As I told Liszt I was only a Sunday musician, he answered me with ready wit, "But Sunday is always a feast day, and you have every right to officiate."

He complimented me upon my piano arrangement, adding that my *pianisme* revealed an experienced musician and a complete command of modern technical science.

He made but one criticism, relative to a passage which could be made easier for the left hand, just where the fingers peck (*picorent*) like birds and the performer's hands cross, as they do in Madame Rimsky-Korsakoff's arrangements. I modified this passage in accordance with his advice.

He questioned me upon the success of my symphony, upon its reception, etc.

I told him that I saw many faults in it myself, that I was often criticised for my want of experience, for excessive modulation, for going beyond bounds, etc. Liszt constantly interrupted me :—

"Heaven forbid! Do not touch it, alter nothing. Your modulations are neither extravagant nor faulty. ('Sie sind wohl sehr weit gegangen—und das ist eben Ihr Verdienst. Sie haben aber nie verfehlt.') You have gone far, indeed, and this is precisely your special merit; but you have never made any mistakes. Do not listen to those who would hold you back; believe me, I entreat you, you are on the right road. Your artistic instinct is such that you need not fear to be original. Remember that the same advice was given to Beethoven and Mozart in their day. If they had followed it, they would never have become masters."

There was nothing for me but to thank him confusedly in French and German.

He asked me about Korsakoff, whom he esteems very highly, and told me of the horrible failure of "Sadko"* at Vienna. Rubinstein, who conducted, said when he brought him the score :—

"Here this work proved a *fiasco*, but I am sure it will be your taste."

In truth it pleased him much, and he thinks a great deal of it.

He asked also about Balakireff and Cui, and wanted news about the performance of "Christus" at the concert of the Free School. When I told him that the choruses went well, but that the *Stabat Mater* could only be given with harmonium instead of organ accompaniment, he said :—

"That is a great difficulty. I shall make some alterations ; the organ must come in with the voices and accompany them throughout."

I told him Korsakoff had had recourse to another method.

"I can guess," Liszt broke in ; "he made the harmonium enter a little before the voices. I know

* "Sadko," symphonic poem.

H

what conducting means. He took a very intelligent course."

Then, changing the subject,—

" It is a pity," he said, showing me "Islamey," *
" that you did not hear this played by your countrywoman, Mademoiselle Véra Timanoff. To-day I have had a musical *matinée*, and she just happened to play this piece."

Afterwards, I was told that when he asked her to play this composition, Liszt had said,— " Mademoiselle Véra, would you kindly decide the Eastern question in your own way ? " She played "Islamey" at the last audience of the Grand Duke. "Do you know," continued Liszt, " that the Grand Duke is well acquainted with Russian music and appreciates it highly. Nevertheless, here in Germany it is evidently not liked. You know Germany ; it is full of composers. I am lost in a sea of music which threatens to entirely submerge me ; but Heavens, how insipid it all is, not one living idea ! With you there exists a vitalising stream. Sooner or later, though probably later, this stream will make a way for itself in Germany."

Then he scolded me like a father for not having published my scores ; this, he said, was indispensable, not only on my own account, but in order that

* Fantasia for pianoforte, by Balakireff.

they might be circulated, they must be performed, etc. He also said to me :—

"Judging from your card you seem to be an authority in chemistry, but how, when and where did you succeed in acquiring so much musical knowledge? Where have you studied? Certainly not in Germany."

When I told him I had never been to any Academy, he began to laugh.

"There you are lucky, dear master," and he added,—"Work, always continue to work. Even if your compositions are not performed, not published, even if they have no success, believe me they will make themselves an honourable way. You have an original talent; listen to no man and work on in your own fashion."

I thanked him for his kindness.

"But I am not paying you compliments," he broke in, with a shade of annoyance. "I am too old to say anything but what I mean. That is why I am not altogether loved here. But can I say that they turn out good music when I find it insipid, and lacking in inspiration and vitality?"

On learning that I was not staying in Weimar, but in Jena, he said :—

"Then we shall meet to-morrow. Where are you stopping?"

Naturally I refused to allow him to visit me,

He then invited me to dine with him at "The Bear," the very hotel from which I had come that morning, and in saying good-bye he again reminded me of his invitation :—

"To-morrow you will be my guest. Do not forget."

I did not venture to ask him to play to me; it would have been too unceremonious.

Naturally I have only given you the sense of his words and, however much I might desire to do so, it would be impossible to reproduce literally, or even to recall, everything that Liszt said in this comparatively short time. He speaks both French and German very fluently, rather loudly, with vivacity, animation and volubility. He might be taken for a Frenchman. He never sits still for a moment, but walks about and gesticulates; there is nothing of the priest about him.

Among other things he told me that Naprawnik's trio had given him much pleasure. At a first reading it struck him as long and wearisome, but after repeated playing he found it excellently written and highly effective. He asked me who had played this trio in Russia. I mentioned Goldstein.

"Don't know him," Liszt interrupted abruptly.

"He is a pianist from the Conservatoire at Leipzig."

" That is no recommendation. They have turned out a number of mediocrities."

He so " enveloped " me, to use your own expression, that in bidding him good-bye I quite forgot to inquire about the dinner to which he had invited me—what time it took place, if it were necessary to dress, etc. I only thought of it when I was in the train. At the station at Jena I met Alexander and Goldstein, who had just come from Leipzig. We went into a little German inn, and there, over several " schoppen " of beer, I had to recount to our young rogues all the details of my interview with Liszt.

The next day found me pensive; I said to myself, how can I go to this dinner ? Perhaps there will be ladies there, and smart people, and I have only my travelling clothes. I resolved to make my excuses to Liszt and to stay away. But how was I to let him know ? It was evident that Liszt would not be staying at "The Bear." He is at home in Jena.

We all three went to the Cathedral. As the concert was to take place there, they would probably be able to inform us at what hour Liszt was to arrive and where he would stay.

To tell the truth, we went without any definite object, and rather on chance. As we drew near to the Cathedral we could hear the tones of the organ. The great door was closed, so we followed a gentleman who entered by a side porch. There were but five people, all told, in the building; Bach's D minor fugue was echoing through the old vaulted roof. We took places and soon saw people beginning to arrive. A shrill voice was heard calling :—

"Now we can begin; gentlemen of the choir, take your places in the gallery at once. We have not much time, and we must look through everything before the Master comes."

We had, by good fortune, hit upon the hour of rehearsal for the concert which was to take place at four o'clock; it was now a little past ten. You can imagine with what pleasure we listened. The performers were perfect. The solos were sung chiefly by Court singers from the Opera at Weimar. The chorus was largely composed of students and members of the Choral Society of the University. No one noticed us. We were neither requested to remain nor to take our leave. Suddenly, about twelve o'clock there was a great commotion near the door.

"The Master is coming, the Master is here!" The organisers of the concert, in their black coats, hastened forward.

The great door was thrown open and displayed the dark and characteristic figure of Liszt in the

dress of an abbé. On his arm was the lady I had
seen in his garden and whom I could not take for
a German.

I was not mistaken. She was the Baroness
Meyendorff, daughter of Gortschakoff, who has been,
I believe, ambassador at Weimar. She is still
young and very attractive in appearance, though
far from being a beauty. A widow, she has made
her home in Weimar, and Liszt lives in her house
like one of the family. He was followed by a
train of pupils, chiefly feminine; the masculine
element was only represented by Zarembski, a
highly-gifted Polish pianist. This galaxy made
their inroad into church without any regard for the
sanctity of the place, chattering in every language,
with a noise resembling a steam saw-mill. Everyone took up their places on the benches. What
element was lacking in this collection? There
were German, Dutch and Polish women, without counting our compatriot, Mademoiselle Véra
Timanoff. It seemed to me Liszt had a special
liking for her. As soon as he had taken his place
near Baroness Meyendorff and the composer Lassen,
he inquired :—

" Where is Mademoiselle Véra ? "

Seeing that she was seated in the last row, he
hastened, without further ceremony, to fetch her
and install her close to him. He listened to the

music with the greatest attention, and most of the
time with closed eyes. When his turn came he
rose and, surrounded by the promoters of the
concert, moved towards the choir. Soon his fine
grey head, bold and energetic, but calm and sug-
gesting perfect self-confidence, appeared at the
conductor's desk.

At a distance he is very like Petroff,* and possesses the same air of superiority and consciousness
of being at home everywhere. He conducts with
his hand, without a baton, quietly, with precision
and certainty, and makes his remarks with great
gentleness, calm and conciseness.

When it came to the numbers for pianoforte, he
descended into the choir and soon his grey head
appeared behind the instrument. The powerful
sustained tones of the piano rolled like waves
through the Gothic vaults of the old temple It
was divine! What sonority, power, fulness!
What a *pianissimo*, what a *morendo!* We were
transported. When it came to Chopin's "Funeral
March" it was evident that the piece was not
arranged. Liszt improvised at the piano, while the
organ and 'cello were played from written parts.

With each entrance of the theme it was something different; but it is difficult to imagine what
he made of it.

* A celebrated Russian singer.

The organ lingered pianissimo on the harmonies in the bars in thirds. The piano, with pedal, gave out the full harmonies, but also pianissimo. The violoncello sang the theme. The effect was prodigious. It was like the distant sound of a funeral knell, that rings out again before the first vibration has quite died away. I have never heard anything like it. And what a crescendo! We were in the seventh Heaven!

Suddenly I recollected my intention of stopping Liszt and excusing myself for not coming to his dinner.

He went out arm-in-arm with the Baroness, surrounded by his suite, who did not hesitate to importune the great master and pay their court to him, undeterred by the least respectful awe.

It was impossible to approach him, so I determined to follow him to the hotel and make my excuses there. Unfortunately it was raining and I got my boots unconscionably dirty. Crossing the threshold I was accosted by Mademoiselle Véra Timanoff, who came up to me gladly and said very gracefully,—" Liszt told us you were in Jena. Have you been here long, etc?" Among other things I mentioned my intention of not going to the dinner.

"Do not think of such a thing," she said; "you would only offend Liszt, who reckons on you. Before we left Weimar he informed us all that you were to dine with him to-day. Come with me!"

Before I had time to protest, Mademoiselle Véra seized my hand and drew me into the multi-coloured circle of her friends.

"Here he is! It is he himself. My fellow-countryman, Herr Borodin;" and she began her introductions: Miss So-and-So, Miss So-and-So, etc. I cannot remember a single name.

"We have plenty of time till dinner. We do not dine till two o'clock. The master has gone to rest; let us go and eat cherries in the meantime," she added.

The mixed crowd streamed into the street carrying me along with it. Having found the cherry-stall, we sat down under a doorway. I was between Mademoiselle Timanoff and a very sympathetic pianist from Düsseldorf. The young ladies spread a piece of paper on their knees, put their cherries on it, and invited me to share the feast. "Help yourself." Alexandrouschka and Goldstein had stopped in front of us, and were surveying this original scene. We fell upon the cherries like schoolboys. We laughed and chattered in every language under the sun. I might have known them for the last century.

At last it was time to return to the hotel, which was not far off. Alexandrouschka and Goldstein were awaiting me there. I called Mademoiselle Timanoff's attention to our young scamps. She cast upon them a swift glance of approbation. After all, we had returned to the hotel too soon.

A special room was reserved for us while dinner was being laid in the dining-room. Without further ceremony the young ladies began to arrange their toilettes and powder their faces before the looking-glasses.

"The Master is still resting. The Master has not come yet," was all one overheard.

Zarembski came up to me and said many pleasant things about my symphony, speaking Russian with a strong Polish accent. He was there with his *fiancée*, a very pretty, but coquettish, young lady from Berlin; both were in the most extravagant get-up, with collars a mile deep, open to impossible depths, wearing hats of a most astonishing shape, from under which issued their long flowing hair. It was a most extraordinary sight; everything about them was done for effect.

Mademoiselle Timanoff, on the contrary, was very simply but tastefully dressed; the German ladies simply also, but not tastefully. Everyone chattered their hardest. At last two o'clock struck and we moved towards the dining-room. The table was laid and decked with flowers.

Liszt made his entrance with the organisers of

the concert, the inevitable Baroness Meyendorff, Lassen, and several others.

"Ah, welcome"! he exclaimed on catching sight of me.

He then introduced me to the Baroness, to Lassen, and to his friend Gille, the chief promoter of the concert. My place was kept on the left hand of Liszt, who took the head of the table; the Baroness sat on his right hand opposite to me. She immediately took the lead in the conversation, related a number of things, and told me that it was she herself who, with Liszt, had played my symphony to the Grand Duke two years ago. Like Lassen she knew every detail of it. Liszt was most agreeable and talked a great deal. He poured out wine for his neighbours and joked with them. He asked many particulars about Russian music, about which the Baroness seemed well-informed. The conversation turned upon opera.

The Baroness said that Rubinstein's opera, "The Maccabees," was not to her taste, that it was colourless and commonplace. She pronounced herself strongly in favour of Rimsky-Korsakoff's "Pskovitaine," * and regretted that it was not performed.

Liszt has not a high opinion of Seroff's operas.

* "La Pskovitaine" ("The Maid of Pskoff"), opera by Rimsky-Korsakoff.

He told us that Seroff desired to have " Judith "
performed abroad, but that he had dissuaded him
and predicted its failure.

" Seroff was evidently very much annoyed with
me," said Liszt, " but I simply told him the truth ;
to my mind, his works lack originality."

He then questioned me with regard to my second
symphony, and asked what success it had won.   I
told him all about it.

" Shall you stay long in Jena ? " he inquired.
" I am going to button-hole you.   Come and see
me again in Weimar ; we will play your symphony."

I assured him I was incapable of playing with him.

" Well, then, the Baroness will kindly play it
with Herr Lassen," he said.   " Have you a good
publisher ?   I will introduce you to Herr Kahnt,
my publisher in Leipzig, he might be of use to you,

And he called Kahnt to introduce him to me.

The dinner passed off quickly and gaily.   On the
other side of me sat one of the Court singers,
Madame Anna Zankow, who was very bright and
animated.

After dinner Liszt again retired to rest.   The
Baroness also disappeared.   We stayed on talking
for a little time, and then directed our steps towards
the Cathedral.   According to German custom, I
wanted to defray my share of expenses, but Liszt
had already paid for everybody.   La Zankow was

very amiable to me, and wrote her name in my pocket-book.

"You must not forget me," she said. In church I had no occasion to trouble about the place I had kept for myself. I remained in Liszt's company. As his name was not upon the bills with those of the other performers, I asked him who would be at the piano. He muttered something under his breath, and said it would be Naumann, an organist who had just come. Why? I have not the least idea. For afterwards we could perfectly well distinguish Liszt's grey head behind the piano, and his rendering of Chopin's "Funeral March" was totally different to what we had heard at the rehearsal. It was evidently an improvisation.

"He always tells his little fibs," said Mademoiselle Timanoff. "He will never admit that he is going to play. He is a curious old man."

At the end of the concert, when the Grand Duke had withdrawn, after having exchanged a few words with Liszt, the public unceremoniously surrounded the master and stared at him unblushingly. Our young friends followed their example. Gille then came up to me and invited me to go to his house with all Liszt's party. In fact, the whole procession set off for his house, which was some distance from the Cathedral. Liszt led the way with the Baroness, we followed with Gille, and the

master's pupils brought up the rear. In spite of
the rain we were accompanied by a compact crowd.
Passers-by, soldiers, students, merchants, officers,
citizens, all respectfully saluted Liszt. Our young
scamps were not ashamed to march by his side and
stare at him without restraint. As we approached
Gille's house a strong odour of pork tickled our
nostrils.

("Es riecht schon nach Bratwûrsten, wir sind
schon da!") "Here we are, we smell the sausages
cooking already," exclaimed the young pupils.

We all invaded Gille's garden, which was
impregnated by the odour of sausages cooking out
of doors. The entrance was gay with flowers, but
Gille was in despair.

"It is done for; we are going to have rain."

The collation was indeed prepared in the garden,
and a fine rain fell incessantly. We dispersed
beneath the arbours into which the tables were
carried. I stayed with the Baroness, who talked a
long time with me. She is a very simple and
amiable woman.

"If you want to hear Liszt," she said to me, "he
is often capricious, and you would not know how
to get him to play, but I will manage it. Except
on certain days I am always at home. Come when-
ever you please, you will always be welcome."

I thanked her heartily; but not expecting to pay

calls, I apologised for having nothing but travelling clothes.

"It is of no consequence," said the Baroness, "come as you are. I entertain in a friendly way; there are no strangers, and I do not like ceremony."

Since that day I have received a quantity of invitations from Weimar. I do not even know from whom; I can only remember one from Mademoiselle Véra, to whom I shall certainly go. I am very anxious to hear her, but I cannot understand how she can play "Islamey," and Liszt's rhapsodies and concertos. She can only strike a minor sixth, her hands are so small.

The time of departure for Weimar came at last. Everybody went to the station. Liszt was evidently tired, and suffered from indigestion; catarrh of the stomach was his chronic complaint. He seemed to have got thinner. The Baroness, Lassen and Gille laid him down in a first-class carriage, where he fell asleep.

In the meantime, unforeseen events took place. There was not room enough in the train and an extra carriage had to be put on; a train had run off the line and they had to wait an hour and a half in the station.

The company seemed depressed for a moment, then recovered its customary animation. The time was spent in drinking beer and laughing. Liszt was asleep.

At last the train moved off and we said good-bye.

Just imagine, similar concerts take place regularly in Jena once a year, whether Liszt is at Weimar or not.

Was it not a piece of luck ? Possibly I might have heard and seen Liszt in Weimar ; but what luck for our young friends, especially Goldstein, who only came from Leipzig the day before and returned the following morning. I shall certainly go and see Liszt, the Baroness and Mademoiselle Véra in Weimar. As to the others, I shall not trouble.

In this way see, my dearest, how an Academician keeps his wedding-day.

We only regretted that you were not with us. But enough of this chatter. Already it is all fading like a dream. One might compare it to the scene of the Venusberg in " Tannhäuser," with Liszt in the part of Venus. As yet I remain under the spell.

I

II.

LETTER TO MADAME BORODIN.

Jena, July 12th, 1877.

I AM going to relate my visit to the *Venusberg*, that is to say, Weimar.

I told you that the Baroness Meyendorff had invited me to hear Liszt under the best conditions possible. I was not long either in getting a line from Gille, who invited me to go over one Sunday and spend the morning with Liszt. But having heard that Liszt was to be in Berlin last Saturday, I concluded that he could not return to Weimar on Sunday, and put off my visit until Monday, remembering that he would be disengaged on that day. At 11.51 I started for Weimar and went straight to Mademoiselle Véra's.

"Why did you not come yesterday morning?" was her first question. "Liszt expected you. He was certain you would come. He played so well!"

I was very much annoyed, but what could be done?

I stayed with Mademoiselle Timanoff until two o'clock, and we had a great deal of music. She played to me—and played exceedingly well—the entire programme of the concert she was giving at Kissingen on the following Friday.

I learned, contrary to my expectations, that Liszt's lessons had for once been put off till Monday.

So much the better, I thought; I will call upon him. And although he sees no one when he is busy, I still had hopes of being present at the lessons.

After dinner I bought a pair of gloves, and as it was too early to visit Liszt, I called on the Baroness Meyendorff.

"What a pity you did not come to Liszt's *matinée* yesterday! He expected you. Gille said you were coming." Such also were her first words.

After chatting an hour with the Baroness, who is highly cultured and an excellent musician, I accepted her invitation to go to tea that evening to meet Liszt.

At half-past four I went to Liszt's, and on the advice of the Baroness I announced myself as somebody come specially from Vienna to take part in the lesson. Otherwise, she assured me that the servant would absolutely refuse me admittance.

I went in. A Dutch pianist was performing a piece by Tausig. Liszt was standing by the piano, surrounded by fifteen pupils.

" Ah! there you are," exclaimed the old master, giving me his hand; "but why did you not come yesterday? Gille assured me that you would not fail to appear. I was very much vexed. I would have shown you that I still have it in me to play Chopin's violoncello sonata."

He then introduced me to his pupils.

" They are all celebrated pianists," he said; " or if they are not yet, they will become such." The young folk all began to laugh. There were all those of both sexes whom I had seen at Jena.

" We have put off our lesson until to-day," said Liszt, " and do you know who is the cause? Little Mademoiselle Véra. She does as she pleases with me. She wished the lesson to be to-day; there was nothing to be done but to put it off."

These words were received with a general burst of laughter.

" But now to work, gentlemen. H., will you play," etc.

The lesson went on. From time to time Liszt would interrupt his pupils, play himself, or make remarks, generally characterised by humour, wit and kindliness, which drew a smile from the young students, and even from the one to whom the

observation was addressed. He did not get ruffled,
or lose his temper, and avoided everything that
might hurt the feelings of the pupil.

"Try to play it *à la Véra*," he said, when he
wanted a pupil to try one of those tricks of fingering to which Mademoiselle Véra was obliged to
have recourse when her hands were too small to
master a difficulty.

He laughed at their want of success. If one of
the pupils said that he could not manage to execute
a certain passage, Liszt would make him sit down
to the piano, saying,—

"Well, now, show us how you *cannot* play it."

In all his familiar observations he used the
greatest delicacy, an extreme gentleness, and
invariably endeavoured to spare the pupils'
dignity.

When it came to Mademoiselle Timanoff's turn,
he made her play his Rhapsody in B minor, which
she was studying for her concert at Kissingen.
After a few little remarks he sat down to the piano
and played a few passages from the piece with his
iron fingers.

"This must be solemn as a triumphal march,"
cried Liszt, springing up from his chair, and putting his arm through Mademoiselle Timanoff's he
paced solemnly up and down the room, humming
the theme of the Rhapsody.

The young people began to laugh.

Timanoff resumed the piece, paying attention to his remarks.   Liszt leaned towards me and said :—

"She is a splendid fellow, that little Véra."

Then addressing himself to her :—

"If you play like that at the concert you will see what ovations ! But they will not be more than you deserve."

Tears of joy ran down Mademoiselle Timanoff's blushing cheeks. Liszt tapped her kindly on the cheek and kissed her on the forehead while she kissed his hand ; this is the custom between Liszt and his pupils.

He has a way of tapping them sharply on the shoulder to attract their attention. All his relations with his pupils are simple and familiar. There is nothing of the professor about him ; he is a father, or rather a grandfather among his grandchildren.

Occasionally, however, a malicious irony lurks in his remarks, especially when he speaks of the Leipzig School.

"Do not play like that," he said to a pupil; "one would think you came from Leipzig. There they would tell you that this passage is written in augmented sixths, and would imagine that was sufficient; but they would never show you how it ought to be played."

And again to a pupil who had just played one of Chopin's studies in a very colourless style :—

"At Leipzig that would be thought very pretty."

Liszt never sets pieces for study; he allows his pupils full liberty of selection. At the same time, they generally ask his advice, to avoid being interrupted, after the first few notes, by an observation of this kind :—

"What a strange taste to play such stuff!"

He does not give much attention to technique or fingering, but occupies himself especially with the rendering and expression. With rare exceptions, however, his pupils possess a great deal of execution, but belong, in this respect, to very different schools.

Liszt impressed me above all by his personality. The lesson lasted two hours and a half. Mademoiselle Timanoff begged Liszt to put off the next lesson from Friday to Saturday, on account of her concert.

"This is the way she always gets over me," said Liszt. "How can I refuse? She is always right, and makes me go her way. Well," he asked the pupils, "are you willing to postpone till Saturday?"

"Yes, yes," was the unanimous reply.

"Well, then, be it so! Till Saturday."

Liszt appeared particularly prepossessed in

favour of Mademoiselle Timanoff.   When she
played really well he exclaimed :—

"Bravo, not one of you can play like this !"

Liszt escorted his pupils to the hall and helped
them to dress.   The ladies kissed his hand as they
took their leave, and he saluted them on the
forehead.   Evidently he has a weakness for the
fair sex.

When we were alone : "What excellent crea-
tures," he said.   "If you only knew what life there
is in them ! "

"If they have life in them, dear master, it is you
who have created it," I replied.

When I took up my hat he asked me where I
was going.   I told him, first to the hotel and afterwards to Baroness Meyendorff's.

"Very good, then we shall meet again.   *Au
revoir.*"

He was evidently tired.

The trains are so awkwardly arranged that I
had to spend the night in Weimar.   The last train
to Jena leaves at 8.20, and I was invited to tea by
the Baroness for half-past eight.

Having secured a room at the Thuringerhof, I
started for the Baroness's house ; Liszt was already
there.   A servant announced that tea was served.
Liszt gave the Baroness his arm and we went into
the dining-room.   The mistress of the house pre-

sented me to her son, aged sixteen, and we sat down to a richly-appointed table, I on the right, Liszt on the left hand, of the Baroness; there were no other guests. The Baroness made tea herself with a kettle and spirit lamp, English fashion. We had all manner of *Zakouski*,* wine and beer, just as we have at home. But the service was much better than in Russia. Liszt talked a great deal. We discussed music.

After tea our hostess led the way to the piano in the drawing-room and gave Liszt one of his own rhapsodies, asking him to show us how such and such passages should be played.

It was a feminine ruse, but an innocent deception; Liszt began to laugh.

"You want me to play it," he said; "very well, but first I want to play Monsieur Borodin's symphony with the composer. Do you play treble or bass?" he asked me.

I refused absolutely.

At last I persuaded the Baroness to sit down to the piano. She consented to play the andante only. Liszt played the bass. How interesting to me was this performance to which I was the sole listener!

But Liszt was not satisfied.

"The Baroness is very kind," he said, "but I

* Cold dishes, generally served in Russia before a meal.

want to play with you. It is impossible that you cannot play your own symphony. You have arranged it so perfectly that I cannot believe that. Sit down there." And without another word he took me by the hand and made me sit down to the bass, he himself taking the treble. I wished to protest.

"Play," said the Baroness, "or Liszt will be annoyed with you. I know him."

I wanted to recommence the andante that was open before me, but Liszt turned over the pages and we attacked the finale, then the scherzo and the first movement. Thus we played the whole symphony with all the repeats. Liszt would not let me rest; after every movement he turned the pages, saying,—

"Let us go on."

When I made mistakes, or omitted anything, Liszt would say,—

"Why did you not do that; it is so fine?" When we had finished he repeated several passages, growing enthusiastic over their novelty and the freshness of the ideas. He subjected my symphony to a most discriminating criticism; according to him, the andante is a perfect master-piece.

"As to form," he said, "there is nothing superfluous; all is fine."

He told me that he had given my modulations as models to his pupils. Referring to one or two specimens, he remarked that nothing like them was to be found in Beethoven or Bach, and that with all its novelty and originality the work defied criticism; it was so complete, so definite and of such a natural beauty. He particularly values the first movement and is very much delighted with its pedal-points, and especially the one on C.

He said nothing particular about the other two movements, but gave me a few practical hints in case I should prepare a second edition; for instance, to write certain passages an octave lower, or *octava*, in order to facilitate the reading.

I recognised in this the results of an exhaustive study of my symphony, in which he had made pencil notes and corrected the printer's errors.

Finally, he told me that I wrote for the piano like a master, and that he was surprised to find I was not a pianist.

"This is not like the symphonies of our composers," he said.

"I know whom you refer to," interrupted the Baroness.

"We know, generally speaking, very little of your music," he added, "but at any rate you see that we have studied it thoroughly."

Liszt and the Baroness then begged me to sing

my romances, or to let them hear something from
" Prince Igor."

"Glinka had no voice," persisted the Baroness,
" yet he sang his own compositions."

To put an end to their entreaties I went through
a short chorus from " Prince Igor," which seemed
to give them pleasure, and then in my turn I
begged Liszt to play something.

Liszt played some of his rhapsodies and a few
other pieces. He did not play much, because it
was getting late; but what a wonderful execution! What expression! What astonishing light
and shade—pianissimo, piano, forte, fortissimo!
What a crescendo and diminuendo, and what fire!

He made me promise to return to Weimar and
let them hear my second symphony. Liszt asked
me if I had no manuscript to show him. It was
arranged that I should return the following
Saturday, that I should attend the lesson at his
house and afterwards go to the Baroness; I was
to stay in Weimar, and be at his *matinée* on
Sunday morning.

At midnight we took our leave, and I escorted
Liszt, whose sight is not good, as far as his door.
Nevertheless, he returned with me to the end of the
street to show me the nearest way to my hotel.

I had heard Liszt under unhoped-for conditions!
I was under a spell and could not sleep. The next

morning I telegraphed to Bessel to send my second symphony and my songs to Liszt; at the same time I wrote to Kranz of Hamburg, who has published them, so I am told, with a German translation. If they come in time I shall take them to Liszt and the Baroness.

Just fancy, in Weimar many people bow to me who do not know me, because they have seen me with Liszt; and the same at Jena.

Thus, my little dove, has your most devoted husband received salvation. Kiss Mascha, Lisa, Gania, etc.

III.

LETTER TO MADAME BORODIN.

JENA, *July* 18*th*, 1877.

LIKE my previous letter, this one will be devoted to the story of my peregrinations in Jena. You remember that Liszt had invited me to be present at his lesson on July 14th, and at his *matinée* on the Sunday following.

The Baroness had asked me to tea on the Saturday evening. On Friday I received a telegram from her, reminding me of this invitation, and begging me not to fail her. Once more I took the 11.51 train, and after having dined called on Mademoiselle Timanoff. Great was my astonishment to find that the lesson had taken place, after all, on Friday. The concert at Kissingen had been postponed, and Mademoiselle Timanoff had requested Liszt to put the lesson back to Friday. The master could not refuse his spoilt child. She has her own way and the old man adores her.

After a few minutes we went to Liszt's house,
Timanoff and I. I had asked her to play me
" Islamey," and she preferred the master's piano,
which had a lighter touch than her own.

" We have pretty well worn it out," she said ;
"let us go to Liszt's; but you must tell him that
you wish to hear me in ' Islamey.' He will make
me play it at once. You will see."

This is, in fact, exactly what happened. It was
sufficient to mention " Islamey " for Liszt to say
at once :—

" My dear Mademoiselle Véra, play us ' Islamey.'
You will see how well she plays it."

Mademoiselle Scheuer, the pianist from Düsseldorf with whom I ate cherries at Jena, happened
to be there, as well as Herr Lutter, an excellent
pianist. Mademoiselle Scheuer was finishing the
last movement of Grieg's concerto, Monsieur Lutter
playing the orchestral arrangement on a second
piano. They were to perform this concerto at the
matinée next day.

As soon as they had finished we were left
alone ; Mademoiselle Timanoff played " Islamey "
admirably, and we began to discuss Rubinstein's
scores, which were lying on the piano. Liszt sat
down to play a few passages from them ; among
others, the overture, the dances, and a few fragments from " Nero."

I told him that the dances in the "Demon" were superior.

"Pass me the score of 'The Demon,'" he said. "I do not know those dances."

He played them all, and even repeated some passages. It reminded me so much of Balakireff's *soirées.*

I was on Liszt's right hand turning the pages for him, Mademoiselle Timanoff was on his left. What a delight to hear Liszt thus, in such a homely way!

He improvised new arrangements like Balakireff, sometimes altering the bass, sometimes the treble notes. By degrees there flowed from this improvisation one of those marvellous transcriptions in which the arrangement for piano surpasses the composition itself. Liszt extemporised for a long time. When we took our leave he detained me.

"We shall meet to-night at the Baroness's," he said. "Come and call for me, will you? We will go together; you will find Zarembski here with me. I wish to go through your symphony with him in your presence, because—"

I could not catch the rest of the sentence which Mademoiselle Timanoff interrupted. I promised to be punctual and we left.

As we walked along I said to Madamoiselle Timanoff:—

" Did you understand what Liszt said to me as we were leaving ? "

" Yes. He wanted to rehearse your symphony with Zarembski, in your hearing, before playing it to-night to the Grand Duke."

" The Grand Duke ? Are we not going with Liszt to the Baroness Meyendorff's to-night ? "

" But do you not know that the Grand Duke has asked to go to the Baroness's to-night to make your acquaintance ? Liszt has talked of you so much to him that, hearing of your arrival in Weimar, the Grand Duke begged Liszt to introduce you to him. How comes it that you do not know ? It was on that account that the Baroness telegraphed to you, so as to be sure of having you."

" What next ! How can I go to an evening reception in a travelling suit ? It is absolutely impossible."

" What nonsense ! " interrupted Mademoiselle Timanoff. " The Grand Duke is simplicity itself. Besides, you can act a part and say you knew nothing about it, since the Baroness has not mentioned it. You can make your excuses ; you can say that you cannot be presented to the Grand Duke in such attire. She will tell you that it is no impediment, and that the Grand Duke is interested in you and not in your costume. She will be responsible for everything ; you will stay and all will go off very well."

I decided to do so, and by eight o'clock I was at Liszt's, where I found Zarembski in a black coat and white tie.

I went through my symphony, Liszt playing bass and Zarembski treble. They played marvellously, especially in the scherzo, where a quantity of details that are generally lost were given due prominence. Liszt, however, made a few slips owing to his failing sight. When they had finished I confided to Liszt my difficulty, and entreated him to excuse me.

"Ah, my dear Borodin," said he, "the Grand Duke values you and not your costume. If Monsieur Zarembski has put on his white tie, it is because he wants to eclipse us both; but you have the best of reasons for wearing your travelling suit, since you have no other clothes."

We laughed, and all three started for the Baroness Meyendorff's.

I enacted my comedy of excuses, and all went off as Mademoiselle Timanoff had predicted. "You are travelling," said the Baroness, laughing, "besides which, we are not in town."

Ten minutes later the bell rang ; we rose, and the Grand Duke made his entrance. He is a tall, middle-aged man. He wore a black frock-coat, a star on his breast, a white waistcoat and pearl-grey gloves. The introductions over, he offered me his hand and gave vent to a string of pleasant phrases which he had been keeping ready for use. He had a profound esteem for our School of Music, was very fond of our music, and was interested in its vitality ; but, so far, he had only had occasion to make the acquaintance of Cui (whom he called Monsieur Coui), and that only very slightly, at Bayreuth ; he was charmed to make mine, etc.

I took refuge in thanks, and everybody moved towards the drawing-room, where stood the piano.

The Grand Duke was accompanied by a certain *Excellenz*, equally bedizened with decorations, and a lady-in-waiting, who kept on her gloves and bonnet the whole evening, even during tea and supper. Was it a rule of etiquette ? I have no idea.

We began with my symphony. I stood by the piano and turned over the pages. The Grand Duke, at a little distance, listened with earnest attention, exchanging glances at the most original and *piquant* passages with Liszt, who was aglow with delight, and in his turn smiled and shot triumphant glances towards me.

When it was over the Grand Duke was profuse in his compliments, and analysed various details of the symphony.

"The highest compliment I can pay you, Monsieur Borodin, is to say that your music, beautiful as it is, does not resemble anything we have heard before. Monsieur Borodin's symphony must certainly be given by the orchestra this year," he added, addressing Liszt. "That can be arranged, can it not?"

Liszt replied that there was nothing to prevent it, if they had the score.

The Grand Duke then requested me to let him hear something from my opera.

It was impossible to refuse. At the request of Liszt and the Baroness I played the little chorus for women, and then the chorus in E minor, "Glory," which was performed at the Free School.

The Grand Duke never ceased repeating: "Charming! highly original! delightful!"

I stopped at length, although the Grand Duke and Liszt wanted me to play the dances. They questioned me about the poem and the orchestration; in short, they showed the greatest interest in my work. They were astonished to find that I was the author of the poem, and were very anxious to hear some of the vocal numbers of the opera.

After having thanked me once more, the Grand Duke rose and offered his arm to the Baroness,

Liszt took the lady-in-waiting, and we all went into the dining-room, where tea was served.

The Grand Duke sat on the right of the Baroness, Liszt on her left; I sat next to the Grand Duke, the lady-in-waiting near Liszt; on my right was his Excellency, then young Monsieur Meyendorff, and Zarembski. The Grand Duke talked all supper-time to the Baroness and myself. He evidently wished to display his knowledge of Russian music and literature. He talked simply and made himself very agreeable.

After tea we returned to the drawing-room in the same order.

Zarembski played a fantasia of his own composition, very interesting, with effects in Liszt's style; then the Grand Duke rose, said a few amiable words to Zarembski and Liszt, thanked me once again, and offering his hand, said in Russian: "Adieu, *au revoir!*" bungling each syllable. His Excellency bowed and followed him out.

After they had left, Zarembski played, exceedingly well, Joseph Rubinstein's very difficult and brilliant fantasia on the " Rhine Daughters."

It was midnight when we went our several ways.

The next morning I rose very early to walk to the residence of the Grand Duke, called The

Belvedere, which is situated outside the town and separated from Weimar by a large park. Suddenly, looking at my watch, I found it was more than half-past ten. Liszt's *matinée* began at eleven, and it was three-quarters of an hour's walk from The Belvedere to Weimar!

It was impossible to find a carriage. I had to step out a good pace, and I reduced the three quarters of an hour to twenty-five minutes, without drawing breath, and under a burning sun. Punctually at eleven I walked into Liszt's house.

There were already a good many people, among others, the Baroness. In the drawing-room, where stood the grand and the upright piano, there were only the ladies and the Grand Duke. But as soon as Liszt saw me he called me and made me pass into the drawing-room through his bedroom.

The *matinée* began. There were more people than chairs; most of the gentlemen had to stand. The ladies were in bonnets, with their parasols in their hands. The men of fashion and the Grand Duke wore black frock-coats, and held their hats; they all carried little walking-sticks, which they never laid aside. Everybody wore gloves. The unfashionable world (like myself, miserable sinner!) were in all sorts of costumes, such as short coats, etc.; with the exception of the Baroness and

Mademoiselle Timanoff, the ladies showed a want
of taste in their dress that was almost grotesque,
although several of them had very handsome
dresses.

Liszt's pupils, male and female, put in an appearance. Liszt accompanied two ladies, who sang
indifferently; but what an accompanist! . . . By
one o'clock all was over.

The pianists were mostly very good, but in very
different styles. Mademoiselle Timanoff was one
of the most striking of them.

After the *matinée* the Grand Duke spoke to me
again, and after paying me a few compliments, said
farewell. Liszt escorted all his guests as far as
the garden.

Timanowa, Zarembski and myself went to dine
at the Hôtel de Russie. Afterwards I went to
Mademoiselle Timanoff's until half-past four, when
we went back to see Liszt, who had promised me
his photograph. He had only just got up, for he
always rests in the afternoon. He asked me to
choose from a packet of photographs.

When I had made my selection, he wrote on the
back: "To Monsieur Alexandre Borodin, in affectionate esteem and sincere devotion. F. Liszt,
July 1877."

I asked for an autograph. He looked through a
heap of music, but found nothing.

"These copies are too bad to offer to you," he said, "but wait a little."

He took a sheet of music paper and wrote upon it the last phrases of his "Divina Commedia," which was not yet printed.

We had often spoken of it in our conversations. As he was evidently tired we took our leave and went to eat ices at a confectioners. There we met some of Mademoiselle Timanoff's friends, who had taken part in the *matinée*. A thunderstorm came on and we were obliged to remain under cover.

Thus the young ladies found time to relate to me a number of intimate gossiping tales, which somewhat astonished me, seeing that I was almost a stranger to them. At 8.22 P.M. I took the train back to Jena.

I V.

LETTER TO MADAME BORODIN.

MARBURG, *July* 22d, 1877.

I HAVE made the acquaintance of a number of professors, and received numerous invitations. I was present at the third meeting of the Naturalist's Society, at which Hæckel, the disciple of Darwin, read a paper upon polynemes and medusæ. I have been to see collections and museums. Finally, I was invited to a *Kneipe* by the students of the Agricultural Institute; my title of quondam professor in the School of Forestry was doubtless my passport to this invitation.

That was a curious evening; students and professors meet on equal terms, as comrades, make speeches, propose toasts, drink beer and clink glasses together. The professors, in particular, are made much of. Some of them were even rather jovial. Comic scenes were enacted; episodes in the life of certain students who were present at the feast were reproduced in shadows on the wall. They were recognised immediately amid peals of Homeric laughter. The subjects of these episodes were not always highly edifying, but did not lack a certain pungency.

But what professors I saw at this gathering! There were some who would have been worthy to figure in a museum or exhibition; one in particular, aged ninety-one, drank his beer, made speeches and proposed toasts!

What is surprising is the order which reigns in the room. A student takes the chair. At the word of command—*silentium! ad loca!*—all is silence and everyone in his place. " It is the turn of Herr " So-and-So," student, or professor, as the case may be.

The silence of the tomb reigns while the orator is speaking, then representations, songs, music, speeches and toasts follow each other as on greased wheels. The words of the songs, copied in a very legible hand, are placed before each guest. Now I understand whence comes the discipline of the German army.

As my road lay through Weimar, I stopped once more at my Venusberg to see for the last time my elderly Venus—Liszt. First I went to bid the Baroness Meyendorff good-bye.

Last Thursday they had received from Bessel all my songs and my second symphony.

The Baroness had read the latter with Liszt the evening before, and seemed very delighted. Liszt intended to have it performed the following day at his *matinée*, when the Grand Duke was to be present. The Baroness invited me to tea in the evening, when Liszt and I were to be the only guests, in order to run through my songs.

From her house I went on to the lesson at Liszt's, who was very pleased to see me again.

"Welcome, dear Borodin," he said. "Yesterday we played your second symphony. Superb!" he exclaimed, kissing the tips of his long fingers.

The lesson was over, but Liszt detained me. He was expecting Zarembski, with whom he wanted to look through my symphony before the *matinée* next day. As soon as Zarembski had arrived, the indefatigable old man sat down to the piano.

"You shall play the andante," he said, "then I shall take your place. I shall render the finale better than you," he added, laughing. And indeed he played the finale with wild and unearthly spirit. I asked him to criticise, to give me his candid opinion and advice; I did not want compliments, I only sought real benefit from his criticism.

"Do not alter anything," he said to me; "leave it just as it is. Its construction is perfectly logical. Generally speaking, the only advice I can give you is to follow your inclinations and listen to nobody.

You are always lucid, intelligent and perfectly original. Recollect that Beethoven would never have become what he was, if he had listened to everybody. Remember Lafontaine's fable—' The Miller, his Son and his Donkey.' Work in your own way and pay no attention to anyone, that is my advice, since you ask me for it."

Then, analysing my symphony in detail, he said that the critics might find fault with me, for instance, for not presenting the second theme of the first movement *amoroso*, or something of that sort, but that they could not pretend in any case that my symphony was badly constructed, having regard to the elements upon which it was based.

" It is perfectly logical in construction," repeated Liszt, passing from one movement to another. " It is vain to say there is nothing new under the sun ; this is quite new. You would not find this in any other composer," continued the great master, instancing such and such a passage. " Yesterday, a German came to call upon me and brought his third symphony. Showing him your work I said, ' We Germans are still a long way from this.' "

He suggested, however, a few little technical criticisms, for a second edition, on the method of adapting it for the piano.

Zarembski prefers my second symphony to my first.

At the Baroness Meyendorff's, in the evening, we three read through nearly all my songs. Liszt accompanied most of the time, while I sang and explained the words. The Baroness preferred " La Reine des Mers," but Liszt thought it too highly spiced.

" It is *Paprika*," * I said.

" No, it is Cayenne pepper," Liszt answered conclusively.

There was a crowd of pianists at his *matinée;* the violinist, Sauret, had just arrived, so that they only played the scherzo from my symphony and not nearly so well as on the previous day. Liszt's sight was bad and he played wrong notes. Besides, he was absent-minded. He was impatiently expecting his daughter, who was to arrive the same day.

In the afternoon I called on Zarembski to hear his fantasia with orchestra, a work in Liszt's style, which shows talent. He consulted me upon the orchestration. Zarembski has really a brilliant future before him as pianist and composer.

Liszt has many talented pupils, but what gave me most pleasure, what really touched me, was that their style of playing the piano reminded me of yours. It has neither the continual restlessness of Goldstein's, nor the affectation of feminine pearli-

* Hungarian red pepper.

ness. Their movements are, as a rule, moderate. Simplicity, breadth and nobility are the qualities personified in Liszt. How I regret that you were unable to hear him !

In leaving, I did not completely cut myself off from him, for from Weimar I went to Marburg, where lived and died the St Elisabeth who inspired the great master.

On the very spot where she was interred, in 1231, her husband erected, first a chapel, and subsequently a cathedral, one of the most elegant examples of the Gothic style, as full of poetry as is the personality of Elisabeth herself depicted in Liszt's work. One may still see the silver reliquary that held her relics, which were scattered to the winds at the time of the Reformation, in order to put an end to the Catholic pilgrimages.*

I forgot to tell you that Liszt's servant took a special fancy to me. I could not understand it at

---

* In an article upon "Liszt in Weimar," published in 1883 in *L'Art*, Borodin recalls the impression felt during this visit to Marburg :—" I had already seen this monument," he writes, " but then it spoke to me only of Elisabeth ; this time her memory was joined with that of the artist who sang of her. The gentle Elisabeth, transfigured, seemed to mingle indissolubly with the grave face of the white-haired master. Both of Hungarian origin, Fate threw them both on German soil ; both belong now to the Catholic Church ; but the sympathy they inspire is neither Hungarian, nor German, nor Catholic ; it draws its source from whatever is great and human,"

all ; one day he made up his mind to ask me in Italian.

"Signor è Russo ?"

"Si, sono Russo e cosa volete ?"

"Ecco ! sono Montenegrino."

"I am a native of Montenegro."

Thence his affection for me. This servant is orthodox, and every Sunday he goes to church to make any number of fanatical genuflexions for the white Czar and for the success of Russian arms in Turkey.

To-morrow I shall start for Bonn, thence to Aix-la-Chapelle ; then I shall go to Heidelberg— my dearly-beloved Heidelberg ! * Afterwards to Strasburg and Munich, where I shall see Erlen-meyer ; then home by Jena and Wilna.

* See the Letter from Heidelberg, page 93.

V

FRAGMENT OF A LETTER TO CÉSAR CUI.

MAGDEBURG, *June 12th*, 1881.

ON the 28th of May (9th of June) I arrived at Berlin from Magdeburg at 10.50 in the morning. One of my travelling companions had advised me to stay at the Kaiserhof, as being the best hotel, and the nearest to the church of St John, where the first concert of the Festival was to take place, so I hired a porter to carry my bag, and started on foot with him. We had hardly left the station when he said to me :—

"There was a festival here yesterday."

"What festival?"

What? You don't know? We welcomed a celebrated guest, the old Abbé Liszt. You have not heard of it? There was quite a crowd—the whole town was at the station. When the old Master arrived he was received with as much enthusiasm as a king; the men waved their hats and the ladies their handkerchiefs, and even their skirts."

Such was the graphic description o my porter.

I learnt, in fact, from Gille, that the evening before an immense crowd had welcomed Liszt at the station with indescribable enthusiasm, and that the ovations had continued until he reached the hotel, where the bands of the local troops had serenaded him.

I will note one more incident, showing with what attentions the venerable master is surrounded. On his alighting at the hotel where the officers usually mess, and where they occupy the best quarters, they unanimously offered to dine in the public room in order to place their dining-room at his disposal.

Having learnt from my porter of Liszt's arrival, I inquired at which hotel he was staying.

" Hôtel Koch," he replied.

"Then take my baggage quickly to the Hôtel Koch," I said.

The hotel was opposite the station. Liszt occupied No. 1 on the first floor. No. 34 on the second floor was at liberty. There I flung down my travelling - bag, found a visiting - card, and went downstairs. Suddenly I came face to face with Spiridion, Liszt's servant. He recognised

L

me at once, overwhelmed me with salutations in
Italian, and flung the double doors wide open
before me ; unannounced, I entered a large room,
in the midst of which stood a Blüthner grand, and
on the piano I at once caught sight of the arrangement of "Antar" for four hands, and the well-
known second edition of the "Paraphrases."

Liszt, near the window, was thanking three
ladies who had just brought him some flowers.
There were already several vases of flowers on
the table, and Liszt was arranging fresh bouquets.
He asked the youngest of the ladies to place one
of these nosegays in a vase, and offered her one in
his turn.

As soon as he saw me Liszt held out both hands
to me, exclaiming,—

"Ah! dear Monsieur Borodin, welcome indeed.
How glad I am to see you, when did you come ?
You will dine with me to-day ? Where are you
staying ? etc. "

And my hands were clasped in his iron fingers
as in a vice.

The ladies, somewhat embarrassed, prepared to
depart, and Liszt took leave of them with many
compliments and thanks. I also showed signs of
going away, especially as I had heard from Liszt
himself that the rehearsal was to take place at
eleven o'clock, and that he expected the town

authorities; but Liszt detained me and asked me to stay and talk with him while he dressed.

"Have you a programme?" he inquired. "Here is one," and he handed me a little red book.

"Look what I have on the desk," said Liszt, showing me a pianoforte score that was lying open; "look at it and admire the way we write here. What do you think of that?"

And Liszt, opening the score at the first page, struck the opening chords of Nicolaï's oratorio, which was lying on the music-desk.

"This is 'Bon-i-fa-ci-us.' Is it not the most trivial Mendelssohnism! That is the sort of music manufactured for us in Germany! But you will hear to-day and judge for yourself. No! you Russians are indispensable to us. Without you I am powerless," said Liszt, smiling. "You have a quick and vital spring within you; the future belongs to you, whereas here it is usually the lifeless corpse. . . . And what are your musicians doing now? I have read Cui's book, and I am much pleased with it. What are Rimsky and Balakireff about? By the way, there is a young compatriot of yours here who gives no bad rendering of Balakireff's 'Islamey.' You shall hear him!"

His faithful valet, Spiridon (Spiridion as the Germans call it), Lazarewitch Kniejewitch, who has been seven years in Liszt's service, urged him to shave and get dressed. But the indefatigable old man would not give in, and continued to overwhelm me with questions.

I tried once more to steal away, but Liszt detained me.

"Come now, you must stay! I am charmed to see you at Magdeburg; I regret not having met you at Baden. Your symphony had an immense success there. You should have heard it; you would have been pleased. It is good for us to do these kind of things in Germany; wakes us up, eh? Now, stay with me; sit down here," he added, observing that I made a move to depart. "You have not yet seen this programme. Read it!"

After numerous reminders on the part of Spiridion, Liszt passed into his bedroom, which adjoined, where the Montenegrin seated him in an armchair and set to work to shave him. Liszt continued to question me in spite of the door between us.

"Come in here; I am not going to act the coy damsel. You will kindly allow me to finish my toilet in your presence, Monsieur Borodin; it will not take long."

I went into his room; Liszt was seated in the armchair; the valet was tying a napkin under his chin, as one does to children lest they should soil their frocks. To the left of the door stood a little table, littered with music that had evidently been thrown off in a moment of inspiration. Involuntarily I bent over it, and saw a score, and beside it a transcription for pianoforte, both in Liszt's autograph, with blots, erasures and cancelled passages.

"Do you know what that is?" said Liszt, without waiting for me to ask. "It will amuse you. I am writing a second 'Valse de Mephisto.' The desire came upon me suddenly; it is quite new. I am busy with the piano arrangement. If you care to see it, take the score. No, not that one," he exclaimed, "it is a bad copy; take this one."

And before I had time, the venerable, grey-headed master escaped from his armchair and the razor of the Montenegrin, his cheeks lathered with soap, and turned over the music until he found another score.

"Here! Look through this."

But this was impossible, for Liszt talked without intermission, asking me if I had brought any manuscript with me, when my symphonies would be published, and if any new works of mine were being performed in Russia.

When I thanked him for his kind collaboration in our "Paraphrases," he laughed, and said:—

"I am exceedingly fond of them. It is such an

ingenious idea! They never lie on the shelf with me."

I mentioned how agreeable and flattering it was to me that he should have written a kind of introduction to my Polka.

"It is only to be regretted," I added, "that Rahter published it without my knowledge, for my own bars of introduction ought to have been left out."

"Oh, no," he said, "do not do that; they are necessary, and must be preserved at any cost, for I wrote the close of my introduction on purpose to dovetail with your few bars. I beg of you not to cut them out."

Hearing me mention "The Steppes" and my quartet, he asked me where they would be published; on learning that I intended them for Rahter, Liszt exclaimed vivaciously :—

"Ah, he is not bad, that Monsieur Rahter; he sent me the 'Paraphrases,' and at the same time he deigned to send me Bach's 'Chaconne,' arranged by my friend Count Zichy; no doubt you have it too. It was charming of him to have published this edition without even asking permission, eh ?"

When I told him that I should like to hear his "Danse Macabre," which I considered the most powerful of all works for piano and orchestra for its originality of idea and of form, for the beauty, depth and power of its theme, the novelty of its instrumentation, its profoundly religious and mystical sentiment, its Gothic and liturgic character, Liszt became more and more excited.

"Yes," he exclaimed, "look at that now! It pleases you Russians, but here it is not liked. It has been given five or six times in Germany, and in spite of excellent performances it turned out a complete *fiasco*. How many times have I asked Riedel to put it in the Society's programmes! He was afraid and could not make up his mind. This time the orchestra seemed much surprised at the first rehearsal, and only became accustomed to it by degrees. If you care for it, you will be completely satisfied. Do you know Martha Remmert? No? She is a remarkable young pianist who plays it admirably; you will judge for yourself, and you will see that I speak the truth."

Speaking of his "Coronation Mass," which was to be performed at the concert, Liszt murmured with contempt: "Yes, no doubt there will be both Coronation and Mass, it was necessary; but we still need a God and a King. I should have preferred the first number only to have been given, in which we have both, and it would have been sufficient; but they wanted to perform the entire work, and it will be rather long."

With regard to "Antar," Liszt told me that at the

first rehearsals the musicians found several passages obscure, but on becoming better acquainted
with the work they caught the spirit of its
masterly orchestration, appreciated it at its real
value, and now performed the symphony with
deep interest.

"You know," he added, "that here, in Germany,
we only grasp music with difficulty, and not at a
first hearing; for that reason works like 'Antar'
need the best possible interpretation."

While we were conversing thus, his toilet was
completed. Spiridion Lazarewitch had just put
the black tie with white edges of a Catholic abbé
round the master's neck and slipped on—not without difficulty—a long, black frock-coat, when the
expected guests were announced.

One of the representatives of the town of
Magdeburg, Major F. Klein, appeared on the
threshold in the uniform of the Prussian Artillery—
a black velvet collar edged with red, epaulettes
fringed with silver, a double row of flat gold
buttons, gloves of chamois leather, his hair oiled
and his whiskers carefully trimmed. Having
saluted Liszt in Teutonic French, the Major
announced that his carriage was at the master's
service to take him to the rehearsal. Liszt introduced us, and as I had not yet got my concert
tickets, which had to be taken at the offices of

the Society, opposite the hotel, the Major was kind enough to accompany me there.

On a table covered with papers, the duties of each member of the committee were written out on little cards with true German preciseness. On being presented with my ticket of membership, I was at once provided with the small red book containing the programme, as well as with tickets for every concert, except the last, which was to take place in the theatre, and for which the tickets were only to be given out the day before.

When the Major and I returned, Liszt was awaiting us on the threshold with Gille. We all four got into the open carriage, Liszt opposite to Gille, the Major opposite me and next to Gille on the back seat. Gille carried the score of the "Coronation Mass."

At the church of St John, where the rehearsal was to take place, rows of chairs were arranged opposite the organ with their backs turned to the altar, for distinguished guests, the managers and the concert committee.

The audience, who faced the altar with their backs to the organ, were fairly numerous, although the rehearsals were not, properly speaking, open to the public

On our entrance there was a general movement

and the whole audience rose to do honour to Liszt.
Liszt bowed as he took his place in the second row
between the Major and Herr Lessmann, a professor
of music at Charlottenburg, and the composer of
some songs which were to be sung at the concert.
Liszt made Gille and myself sit in the first row, in
order that we might follow the score. The first
number on the programme, a Symphony for organ
and orchestra, was over, and the rehearsal of the
"Coronation Mass" had begun. Liszt listened
with lowered head, closing his eyes from time to
time. Now and then his lips moved and he
murmured his remarks to himself, or communicated them to us, commenting upon various passages of the work itself, or upon its execution.
On reaching the Gradual, Liszt bent towards me to
explain that this portion, which is often left out
in other Masses, is obligatory in the "Coronation
Mass," and that the use of fourths constitutes a
characteristic feature of Hungarian music. Most
of Liszt's observations were distinguished by
his habitual *bonhomie* and humour. Suddenly
he became serious, and said at intervals: "But
that is not right."

No longer able to endure it, he jumped up from
his seat and went towards the choir. He had
hurt his leg a short time before and limped
slightly. Leaning upon the Major, the veteran

stepped forward vigorously, and soon his white head appeared over the conductor's desk.

After explaining his wishes to the leader and the band, he made them repeat the passage, and never rested or returned to his place until the double basses and violoncellos had succeeded in playing their pizzicati passages as they were written, not simultaneously with the chord, but one crochet-beat later.

After the "Coronation Mass" came the famous "Bonifacius," the oratorio by Nicolaï, Capellmeister at the Hague, which had been given a short time previously at Cologne, and which, as I have said above, was the object of Liszt's aversion. They all made fun of this "Bonifacius," and someone, I think it was Lessmann, declared it was not "Bonifacius," but "Malefacius." Gille, Liszt's intimate friend since 1840, and an enthusiast for modern music, who reminds me of Stassoff by his vivacity and the brusqueness and freedom of his sarcasms, leaned towards me and said :—

"Now you are going to have a treat! You are going to watch the winding of a skein! It will try the patience of the audience, but, thank goodness, one duet will be cut out. I cannot listen to such music with equanimity. It trails along like a tape-worm. Why the deuce do the committee pursue such a line and stand so on ceremony?

Why do they let such works figure in the programme? We have had enough of them. Let
the composers swear or rage, so much the worse
for them. Such timidity! Such pottering! It
is bad and there is an end of it. In matters of art
a sense of fitness is essential; it is on that score
that I am always at variance with my colleagues."

Silence reigned. The composer of "Bonifacius"
had seated himself next to Liszt, who held the
pianoforte score of the oratorio. Liszt held his
tongue, or occasionally let drop remarks of this
nature :—

"The triplets of the violins and the alto do not
come out loud enough, we do not hear them; but
perhaps, with a larger audience, the acoustic conditions will improve."

Nicolaï did not seem satisfied with his success.
Without waiting till the end, Gille gave me the
score of the "Coronation Mass," begged me to tell
Liszt that he had been obliged to return to the
office, and fled. I suspected him of not having
patience enough to sit through this "winding of
the skein" without being allowed to let off a single
bad word, because Liszt and the composer were
sitting just behind him.

It was dinner-time when we returned; the table
was laid and the room full of people. Liszt's
place was distinguished by a crown of laurels, and

a huge bouquet of flowers was placed in front of him. The company had already sat down to table. The dinner was very merry and animated; Liszt was toasted enthusiastically, and responded by drinking to the committee and other persons present.

After dinner, Liszt went to lie down as usual; this was the more necessary as the concert was fixed for half-past six o'clock, and the day was to be succeeded by four equally busy ones.

At the concert in the evening he sat in the first row, between Gille and the Major, and afterwards near his pupil, Martha Remmert, a blonde and good-looking German, whose lips were faintly shaded with down. She was tall and graceful, slightly affected, and with a touch of coquetry. Opposite to Liszt was a row of ladies seated on the church benches. (As I have already explained, these benches, which were fixed, had their backs turned to the organ, while the chairs faced it.) On the chairs were seated, besides Liszt and the members of the committee, the performers, composers, reporters, authorities, etc. Although I was not a member of the committee, I was invited to take my place in the first row, near to Major Klein and to Liszt. This was a very favourable position for seeing everything. The public and the members of the Society were seated on the benches. I could see at less than a yard from me, everyone who approached Liszt.

The public in the front row stared at Liszt and his neighbours, made remarks, followed Liszt's slightest movements, and even tried to overhear his conversation. When, on seeing Mademoiselle Remmert bow to him as she moved towards her place, Liszt stopped her and made room for her to sit down by him, with that sweet and caressing smile which is so characteristic of him, the ladies near flushed with spite, and glared shamelessly at the fortunate Remmert, and never ceased, during the whole concert, to smile and cackle, while they devoured her with envious glances. Liszt chatted to her good-naturedly, thereby only increasing the anger of these dames. Mademoiselle Remmert gave me at first an impression of affectation, but, as soon as I knew her better, I was convinced that it was merely external. As a pianist she is of the first rank, as regards energy, vigour, expression and rhythm. After hearing her rendering of the " Danse Macabre," and afterwards of the first movement of Liszt's sonata, I was astonished at the contrast between the coquettish and affected German girl and the pianist in petticoats.

Her large hands, almost masculine, have a man's touch, and with one's eyes shut one could hardly believe that one was listening to a woman, much

less to a young girl. This contrast was noticeable
in other respects. In spite of her external appearance, she was really a very energetic girl, struggl-
ing bravely against the trials of life and against
the poverty brought upon her family by a drunken
bully of a father. In spite of this she educated
herself well enough to enter as governess into a
rich family in Vienna; while at the same time
attending to the education of her sisters, she carried
her own to the point of becoming a first-class
pianist.

At the Magdeburg Festival she was to play
Liszt's "Danse Macabre." This explains quite naturally the marked predilection which he displayed
for her, to the great disgust of the envious ones.

The concert opened with a symphony for organ
and orchestra by Charles A. Fischer, organist of
the New Town Church at Dresden.

. . . .

The second number consisted of Liszt's "Coronation Mass," given for the first time, June 8th, 1867,
at Budapest, when the Emperor Franz Joseph I.
and Elisabeth of Austria were crowned apostolical
King and Queen of Hungary. The music of this
Mass is enchanting almost throughout; the "Credo"
is superb in its depth and religious severity. It
bears the stamp of the old Catholic liturgy, being
in the Dorian Mode with almost continuous unisons,

as in the chants of our own Greek Church. The "Offertory" is a fine orchestral piece in Liszt's new style; the "Benedictus" with a violin solo is also good, as are many of the other numbers. But the "Credo" surpasses everything else. It was a great artistic enjoyment to me to hear this Mass.

An interval of ten minutes; then a portion of an organ concerto in B major, composed and played by Th. Forschhammer, organist and musical director at Quedlinburg. Respectable music, but nothing striking; execution ditto. It lasted twenty weary minutes.

The last number on the programme was the second part of the oratorio by Nicolaï, director of the Music School at the Hague, that wearisome academical production which I have already mentioned. Fortunately the first number was cut out— the "Chorus of Heathen Maidens." This cut was not made from musical considerations, but because the local clergy objected to the performance of a pagan chorus in a Protestant church. Their conservatism was not, however, consistent; for while they refused to allow the heathen maidens to sing, they placed no such prohibition on the heathen men. Was it after all a protest against the emancipation of women? But after allowing the pagan priest to sing, they gave the same permission to his daughter, and also to a chorus of dryads, who are not, as far as I know, in any way connected with the Lutheran faith. We must do this justice to the composer—his " Bonifacius " is long and extremely wearisome. My German Stassoff, Councillor Gille, could not restrain himself. Leaning backwards, behind Liszt and the other people who divided us, he said to me in a low voice : " Now comes the tape-worm. Listen well ! "

This remark was in connection with the wearisome duet between the daughter of the pagan priest and Bonifacius. Liszt was evidently tired ; he was bored, he dozed, and even went to sleep. This often happens to him when, in spite of his fatigue, he thinks himself obliged, for some reason or other, to remain until the end of a concert. Moreover, he sleeps very cleverly, bending his head, closing his eyes and pursing up his under lip. Then he begins to snore, as he does even when awake while listening attentively. Outsiders might believe him to be entirely absorbed in contemplating the beauties of a musical work. To conceal the fact that he is simply sleepy and hears nothing, Liszt beats time on his knee with one finger, or pretends to be following the performance of the piece on the piano.

The hypnotic condition suggested by " Bonifacius " passed off after the concert. All Liszt's intimate friends assembled in the dining-room of

M

the hotel, round the master, who presided at the
supper and had become once more the gayest,
wittiest and most amiable company, eating and
drinking with good appetite, chatting, joking
incessantly, and saying the most brilliant things.
The supper went off gaily and noisily. Naturally
there were toasts in honour of the hero of the day.
The naughty old man, a great admirer of the fair
sex, had placed on either side of himself the pianist,
Martha Remmert, and the singer, Fräulein Breiben-
stein of Erfurt; he paid them assiduous court, as
usual. Liszt remained until midnight, and most
of the guests left with him.

The next day, June 10th, Liszt expressed a wish
to show me his new " Valse de Mephisto" before
the rehearsal. He was also expecting several
singers, with whom he wished to go through some
of the vocal passages. From ten o'clock in the
morning his apartment was never free from
visitors.

I could not go to him, however, as I was obliged
to attend the orchestral rehearsal in order to give
the conductor, Herr Nikisch, a few hints with
regard to the performance of " Antar "—(the cadenza
for harp, the character which the wind instruments
ought to give to the Oriental themes, etc.).

The rehearsal, as well as the concert, was to take
place almost in the outskirts of the town, at the

Odéon, a dancing-saloon of a truly democratic character. There was no hall sufficiently large in Magdeburg, and it was necessary to put up with this one, in spite of its distance.

The rehearsal was fixed for 10.30 A.M. At the time appointed, I went there on foot in a heavy shower. I arrived much too soon; the audience was already fairly numerous, but the musicians had not all arrived. A band of women, of no very high order, were carrying double-basses and violoncello cases on their shoulders, in truly patriarchal style. The room was built of wood, like our railway stations, not very lofty, with a gallery and two side boxes; below, an amphitheatre, with rows of chairs in the middle, and a low stage for the orchestra; all this was painted brown with the exception of the stage, which was in its primitive nakedness. The conductor was provided with a sort of tribune in the form of a wooden case.

The room was hung with simple garlands of greenery, and decked with escutcheons bearing the arms of Magdeburg, a stone tower crenulated at the four corners.

A buffet adjoined, and under the gallery were a few tables decked out here and there with *bocks* and *appetitsbrödchen* (sandwiches) for the enjoyment of the members of the orchestra.

In the corners of the room, groups of people were

discussing the details of the concert and the works which figured in the programme, the performance of the day before and the town scandals. Some were yawning and looking at their watches, but everybody awaited with patience, and good-humouredly, the arrival of the conductor and the beginning of the rehearsal.

I asked permission from the President of the Society, Professor Riedel, to pass on to the conductor, before the rehearsal commenced, a few suggestions from Rimsky-Korsakoff with regard to the harp-cadenza, etc.

" Herr Nikisch," he replied, " has not come yet, but we can simplify matters. Wait a moment ! "

Monsieur Riedel called the players to whom the suggestions of Rimsky-Korsakoff were addressed, and introduced them to me, saying :—

" Professor Borodin desires to communicate to you the wishes of the author of ' Antar ' with regard to several passages in his symphony."

The musicians listened to my remarks with admirable attention. The harpist informed me that he already performed the cadenza in accordance with the composer's wish—probably by the help of annotations made by Korsakoff in the part for harp, for I cannot account for it otherwise.

I was anxious to know how the part for horn in

A flat in Berlioz's " Queen Mab " scherzo would be performed. I questioned Riedel on this subject. He immediately called the third horn, who told me he played it as it was written, in A flat; he took off, for me to look at, a little crook in A flat, and replacing it, performed the entire passage as I had requested. Observing that I was interested in the orchestra, and that I showed a certain knowledge of it, the players surrounded me and began to talk to me of various details in the execution of the programme. Whilst waiting for the conductor, Professor Riedel introduced me to a great number of musicians of more or less repute, belonging to Magdeburg and other places. I discovered that my name was well-known in the musical world, thanks to the performance last year (1880), at Baden-Baden, of my symphony in E flat major. I had to undergo a shower of compliments with regard to this symphony. Some had heard it, others knew of it through articles in the newspaper or by the arrangement for piano; no one seemed entirely ignorant of it.

At last there was a movement among the orchestra; the conductor had arrived. He was half an hour late. Really, I begin to ask myself, where is that German punctuality which is so often flung in the face of us Russians. I must also record a piece of carelessness, a defect which we are pleased to attribute to the Slavonic rather than to the Teutonic race. The orchestra was not the same as on the previous day; instead of the forty-six players from the Magdeburg theatre, and the local military bands, to-day it was the renowned band of the Leipzig theatre (Gewandhaus), reinforced, and consisting of twelve first violins, eleven second ditto, eight violas, eight 'cellos, eight double-basses, three flutes, two oboes, without counting an English horn, two clarinets and a third bass clarinet, three bassoons, four horns, four trumpets, three trombones, one tuba, instruments of percussion, and harp; in all, an orchestra of seventy-four musicians, besides several military instruments, especially engaged for Wagner's "Kaisermarsch." Add to these the choral masses to come, the soloists and a huge concert-grand by Blüthner.

This was known beforehand; it had all been announced long ago on the programmes, with a detailed list of the performers, and yet the organisers had not troubled to find out that the stage could not be made to hold more than two-thirds of this mass, even supposing that the Leipzig band played standing, and without seats.

Then began a general scrimmage in the orchestra. First the chorus had to leave the platform, then the unhappy double-basses and the piano were pushed from place to place. The musicians were crowded together like a flock of sheep chased by the shepherd's dog; in altering the position of the music desks, one unfortunate second violin fell off the platform as well as his instrument, and measured his length on the floor, luckily without serious results to either. It reminded me of the fable by Kriloff, " The Quartet."

" Thou, my little Michael,* place thyself with thy double-bass opposite to the viola, and I will sit opposite the second-violin."

Only the eight 'cellos were allowed to sit down; all the remainder had to stand, the bows flashing like infantry bayonets, and the bells of the brass instruments protruding between heads.

This hubbub lasted a whole hour, from eleven till twelve o'clock. What struck me most was, that in spite of all there was no grumbling, not a word of complaint, not a gesture of impatience; here was German discipline and obedience in full force.

Finally Nikisch appeared at his desk and raised his baton. For a long time he stood as if petrified in this cataleptic attitude; at last he waved it briskly and away we went.

Unfortunately, they only rehearsed Wagner's " Faust " overture, fragments of " Romeo and Juliette," and the " Kaisermarsch "; the two first of

---

* The name Michael is applied to the bear in Russia, as Martin is in France.

those pieces were gone through on account of a new bassoon player, who did not belong to the Leipzig orchestra, and the last on account of the chorus and military instruments having to take part in it. All the rest had been thoroughly got up already at Leipzig. . . .

(Here the letter broke off and was never finished.)

VI.

LETTER TO MADAME BORODIN.

WEIMAR, *June 19th*, 1881.

I ASK your pardon for not having written, chiefly for want of time. I left Magdeburg on June 14th, at eleven in the morning, not for Leipzig, but—forgive me—for Weimar, for my *Venusberg*. Apart from my white-haired Venus I was also attracted by the last entire representation of Goethe's "Faust," the first and second parts, given on two consecutive evenings, each performance lasting from half-past five to eleven P.M. It is excessively long, but is put on the stage in a most original manner; the scene is divided into three platforms, so that, without lowering the curtain, the action passes from heaven to hell, from Gretchen's room to the garden, etc. There I understood for the first time how far the drama "Faust" surpasses the opera. The wit, the satire, the humour, the depth of sentiment stand out clearly in the drama. In the opera there is nothing of all this. I came to the conclusion that Faust should always be played in German; the part of Gretchen, especially, should be rendered by a German woman. Devrient is perfection itself in the part of Mephistopheles. The incidental music is by Lassen; probably it would be better without this music.

But I am wandering from my subject. I shall not tell you anything about the festival at Magdeburg, of which the programme alone filled a whole pamphlet, and an account of which would demand a volume. I shall only tell you that "Antar," except for trivial alterations of time in two places, was admirably performed, infinitely better than with us, as regards sonority. The interpretation, the clearness, the light and shade, were surprising. Nikisch is an excellent conductor, who had so far assimilated "Antar" as to be able to conduct it without score. The first two movements were least appreciated, while the third and, to my great astonishment, the fourth were loudly and unanimously applauded. On the whole, opinion was very favourable to "Antar," which positively won some success. The doings of our musical school are more talked of here than I could have believed. My symphony has won for me such a reputation in the German musical world, that I hardly need mention my name to receive the most flattering compliments :—

" Then you are the composer of that excellent symphony which had such a great success at Baden-Baden last year ? "

I have had even to give my autographs as souvenirs. One of these I wrote on a wooden fan for some young ladies I met in the hotel dining-room, who were total strangers to me. It is incredible, but people here pay court to me, and I am within measurable distance of being canonised. Of course, I am not speaking of Liszt and the Baroness Meyendorff; but the singers, pianists and musicians of Magdeburg almost wore me out with compliments. Herr Riedel is a good-hearted fellow, and we have become as friendly as if we had known each other for a century. His daughters, who, like Frau Riedel, are young and charming, made as much of me as if I had been one of the family. On the day of my departure I presented them with flowers and sweets, in remembrance of their kind hospitality in having acted as my *ciceroni* in Magdeburg.

Scharwenka, the Berlin pianist, who married a Russian lady, Madame Zinaïda Petrowna (from Wiatka), made me promise to stop in Berlin and spend a few days with him on my return to Russia.

English, Americans, and heaven knows who besides! are incredibly friendly to me; in short, I am perfectly spoilt; I live in clover. I really feel ashamed of it.

Liszt is a real Balakireff. What a true-hearted man! There, as you would say, are "really friendly friends." Fancy, on my arrival at Weimar he inquired where I was staying.

"Probably at the Russicher Hof?" he said. I had hardly had time to tell him that I did not like that hotel, and that Lutter, the pianist from Hanover, had advised me to take a room in a private house, when the friendly old man hastened to say :—

"But Lutter has not come yet. Wait a little, I will find you a lodging."

Then calling his servant :—

"Pauline! Pauline! We must find an apartment in a private house for Herr Borodin. Go and enquire at No. So-and-So and So-and-So," and he began to enumerate a series of addresses. "Ten years ago I would not have let you go at any cost and you would have been my guest; but now-a-days, you see, I am lodged like an old maid; where could I find room for you?"

I endeavoured to thank him and to excuse myself in every way for troubling him, but I was obliged to await the return of Pauline, who had found me a small room, very clean and *freundlich* as the Germans say. Under my windows is the garden of Goethe's house; on the other side is a garden through which I can get to Liszt's; about twenty yards away is the Grand Duke's Park, and everywhere one's ear is filled with the song of the nightingale. Close at hand I have Liszt and the Baroness Meyendorff, who is always charming to me.

In taking leave of me, Liszt said,—

"To-morrow, at eight in the morning, I shall pay you my formal call, as I wish to see if you are comfortably housed."

He was much pleased with my "Steppes," and urged me to arrange it for four hands by the following day.

"Wait, I will get you some paper. Spiridion, bring me the music-paper I have there." But without waiting for his order to be carried out, my Balakireff stumped off with heavy steps to search the cupboard, and produced a sheet of paper upon which he himself inscribed *primo* and *secondo* with a bit of pencil. What will you think of me? I forgot this piece of paper and was not able to go back for it.

The following morning, between eight and nine o'clock, just as I had gone out to get my early coffee, the dear old fellow brought it himself and left it with his card. I found both on my return and went off to his house at once to thank him for his thoughtfulness and attention.

"Well!" replied my Venus of the white locks, "it is because I want you to set to work upon the pianoforte arrangement."

Under various pretexts he was always enticing me to him and the Baroness. The following day he told me that Prince Wittgenstein had sent me a pressing invitation to go to his house with Liszt and the Baroness, and that the Grand Duke, who desired to see me, would be there, and also his daughters.

"I will call for you at nine o'clock to-night," Liszt concluded.

I endeavoured to decline this latest attention, pointing out that he was lame, and that it was I who ought to call for him.

"Do not oppose me," dear Monsieur Borodin. "Let me do what I think right. I shall call for you at nine P.M.," added my obstinate old Balakireff.

It was a case of putting on evening dress, white tie, black coat and opera hat. But chance alone had brought me to Weimar, and I had not the necessary equipment; however, no sooner had Liszt's pupils heard of the case than one lent me his hat, another helped to tie my evening bow, and even came to my rooms with his wife, an English lady, to inspect me from head to foot. At last my

Balakireff arrived. Catching sight of my transcription of " Les Steppes," which was half-finished,
he exclaimed :—

" Here they are at last, your famous camels !
Come, we will take this with us and play it at the
Wittgensteins," and the old man folded the music
and slipped it into his pocket. I entreated him to
abandon the project, saying that the transcription
was not finished, and that we could not possibly
play it without looking through it first; but he
became irritable.

" Do not vex me," he said, " you shall thump the
bass and I will bang the treble, and it will go
splendidly; the latter part you must thump by
yourself."

And the obstinate old gentleman actually did as
he threatened. At the Wittgensteins we played
the first portion as a duet, and I had to finish it
alone.

When shortly afterwards I showed him the
complete transcription, I asked his opinion upon a
passage that was somewhat difficult for me.

" Leave it as it is," he answered. " If Monsieur
Borodin cannot manage it, Madame Borodin will
do so with ease. Give her my compliments and
tell her what I said."

I should mention that in course of conversation
I had told him you were a good pianist. I dedi-

cated " The Steppes " to Liszt.   He embraced me
and thanked me warmly.

I shall endeavour to return as soon as possible.
Happy as I am here, my heart aches for you all; I
am ashamed to be enjoying myself so much while
I know you are in such trouble.

WE get a complete picture of Borodin in these hurriedly-written letters. We find in them all the simplicity of the man and the sincerity of the artist.

We see also the grand personality of Liszt in a new light; and Borodin may be said to have added another precious page to the biography of this master, whose influence upon modern art has not always received the appreciation it deserves.

Borodin's modesty must have been occasionally hurt by the eulogies that were bestowed upon him, and it is only to the intimate nature of this correspondence that we owe the confession of the praises he received.

Liszt went to his grave only a few months before Borodin. He now lies by the side of Jean Paul, in the cemetery of Bayreuth, beneath the humble wooden cross that alone may distinguish the grave of one of the Franciscan order.

The town of Bayreuth has erected above this cross a romanesque chapel, designed, it is said, by young Siegfried Wagner.

The severe style of this chapel does not jar with

the simplicity of Liszt's humble monument, and seems only to have been erected as a shelter for the innumerable memorials which were sent to Liszt's funeral from all parts of the world.

Among the most prominent is a silver crown, bearing the following inscription in enamel :—

TO THE MEMORY OF

F R A N Z   L I S Z T.

From the Russian composers and admirers of his genius.

Messieurs BALAKIREFF, BORODIN, BLUMENFELD, GLAZOUNOFF, CUI, LIADOFF, LIAPOUNOFF, LADIJENSKY, RIMSKY-KORSAKOFF, SCHTCHER-BATCHEW, DUTCH, BELAÏEFF, D. STASSOFF, W. STASSOFF.

Mesdames SCHESTAKOW, MOLAS, RIMSKY-KORSA-KOFF, STASSOFF.

Borodin's correspondence reveals to us the secret of this profound gratitude which the whole of the modern Russian school of music desired to express to this master, who was the first in Western Europe to make known its works, just as in Germany he was the first to reveal the genius of Richard Wagner.

CATALOGUE OF THE WORKS OF BORODIN.

1. *First Symphony,* in E flat major (1862-1867). (St Petersburg, B. Bessel & Co.) (1) Adagio. Allegro moderato. (2) Scherzo. (3) Andante. (4) Molto allegro. Arranged for pianoforte (four hands), by the composer. Arrangement of the *andante* for two hands by Th. Jadoul.

2. *Four Songs,* with French words, by Paul Collin. (Moscow, Jurgenson.) (1) La Princesse Endormie (ballad), 1867. Transcription for pianoforte (two hands), by Th. Jadoul. English words by E. Carrick, German by H. Von Ahringen. (Leipzig, Wild.) (2) Mon Chant est Amer et Sauvage. (3) Dissonance. (4) La Mer (ballad), 1870. Transcribed for pianoforte (two hands), by Th. Jadoul. German text by V. Dwelshauvers-Dery. (Leipzig, C. Wild.)

3. *Four Songs.* (St Petersburg, B. Bessel & Co.) (1) Chanson de la Forêt Sombre. (2) Fleurs d'Amour. (Heine.) French words by P. Collin. (3) La Reine des Mers. (Ditto.) (4) Le Jardin Enchanté.

4. *First Quartet,* in A major, on a theme of Beethoven, dedicated to Madame Rimsky-

Korsakoff. (Hamburg, Rahter.) (1) Moderato.
(2) Andante con moto. (3) Scherzo. (4) Andante.
Allegro risoluto. Arranged for four hands, pianoforte, by the composer. Arrangement for two
hands, of the scherzo, by Th. Jadoul.

5. *Second Symphony*, in B minor (1871-1877)
(St Petersburg, B. Bessel & Co.) (1) Allegro
moderato. (2) Molto vivo. (3) Andante. (4)
Allegro. Arranged for pianoforte (four hands) by
the composer.

6. *Paraphrases*, twenty-four variations and
fourteen little pieces for piano, on a favourite
theme . . . dedicated to little pianists who can
execute the theme with one finger of each hand,
by A. Borodin, C. Cui, A. Liadoff and N. Rimsky-
Korsakoff. The polka, Marche Funèbre, and
Requiem, are by Borodin. (Hamburg, Rahter.)
Ditto. Second edition, with an Introduction by
Liszt to the polka by Borodin.

7. *Dans les Steppes de l'Asie Centrale.* Symphonic sketch, 1880. (Leipzig, Belaïeff.) Arranged
for pianoforte (four hands), by the composer. Arranged for two hands by Th. Jadoul.

8. *Petite suite* for pianoforte (two hands), dedicated to Countess Mercy-Argenteau (1885). (St

Petersburg, B. Bessel and Co.) (Au couvent, Intermezzo, deux Mazurkas, Rêverie, Sérénade, Nocturne.)

9. *Scherzo*, in A flat major, for orchestra, dedicated to Th. Jadoul. Arranged for two hands by the composer. Arranged for four hands by Th. Jadoul.

10. *Septet*, for voices and pianoforte, dedicated to Countess Mercy-Argenteau (1886). (Liége, Vᵉ. Léopold Muraille.)

11. *Quartet* on the name B-la-f, by Rimsky-Korsakoff, Liadoff, Borodin and Glazounoff. (Leipzig, Belaïeff.)

3. *Serenata alla Espagnola*, by A. Borodin. Arranged for four hands, pianoforte, by the composer. Arranged for two hands by Th. Jadoul.

———

POSTHUMOUS WORKS.

12. *Second Quartet*, in D minor, dedicated to Madame Catherine Borodin. (Leipzig, Belaïeff.) (1) Allegro moderato. (2) Scherzo. (3) Notturno. (4) Andante vivace. Arranged for four hands by S. Blumenfeld.

13. *Prince Igor,* opero in four acts, with pro-logue ; completed by Messieurs Rimsky-Korsakoff and Glazounoff. (Leipzig, Belaïeff.) Orchestral score ; pianoforte and vocal score. German and French versions. Arranged for piano by Messieurs S. and F. Blumenfeld, Glazounoff, Dutch, Sokoloff, Monsieur and Madame Rimsky-Korsakoff. Over-ture, dances and march, arranged for pianoforte by N. Sokoloff.

15. *Arab Melody* for voice and piano. Words by Borodin. " Si tu fuis mes Regards." French translation by Madame Alexandrow. (Leipzig, Belaïeff.)

15. *Melody* to words by Pushkin, " Dans ton pays si plein de Charmes." French translation by Madame Alexandrow. Composed in 1881 on the death of Moussorgsky. (Leipzig, Belaïeff.)

16. *Sérénade de Quatre Galants à une Dame* humorous quartet for male voices. French trans-lation by Madame Alexandrow. (Leipzig, Belaïeff.)

17. *Song,* words by Count A. Tolstoi. " La vanité march en se gonflant." (Leipzig, Belaïeff.)

18 *Chez Ceux-là et Chez Nous,* song with orches-tral accompaniment. Words by Nekrassoff. French version by J. Sergennois. (Leipzig, Belaïeff.)

Arranged with pianoforte accompaniment by G. O. Dutsch.

19. Two movements of the *Third Symphony*, unfinished, in A minor, orchestrated by A. Glazounoff. (Leipzig, Belaïeff.) (1) Moderato assai. (2) Vivo. First movement arranged for pianoforte (four hands) by A. Glazounoff; the second movement by N. Sokoloff.

20. *Finale of Mlada*, an unfinished opera-ballet. Orchestrated by Rimsky-Korsakoff. French version by J. Ruelle. (Leipzig, Belaïeff.) Arranged for four and eight hands by N. Sokoloff.

THE END.